WALK
LIKE A
MAN

Robert J. Wiersema

WALK LIKE A MAN

Coming of Age
with the Music of
Bruce Springsteen

The Robson Press

First published by Greystone Books, an imprint of D&M
Publishers Inc., 2323 Quebec Street, Suite 201, Vancouver, BC,
V5T 4S7

This edition published in Great Britain in 2012 by
The Robson Press (an imprint of Biteback Publishing Ltd)
Westminster Tower
3 Albert Embankment
London SE1 7SP

ISBN 978-1-84954-402-3

10 9 8 7 6 5 4 3 2 1

A CIP catalogue record for this book is available from the
British Library.

Printed and bound in Great Britain by
CPI Group (UK) Ltd, Croydon, CR0 4YY

For Peter, Greg, and Colin
Blood brothers against the wind...

And for Derek
Missing. Missed.

WALK
LIKE A
MAN

Now I'll do what I can
I'll walk like a man
And I'll keep on walkin'
BRUCE SPRINGSTEEN, "Walk Like a Man"

"Meaning is a communal cocktail."
BRUCE SPRINGSTEEN, Mojo magazine, 2010

Contents

Introduction

certain songs, they get so scratched into our souls
THE HOLD STEADY[1]

Y OU KNOW THOSE mornings where you wake up and
feel paralyzed, crushed by the weight of the world? I
had one of those mornings the other day. It was a perfect storm of things: my job at the bookstore always goes nuts in
September, and I was scrambling, falling further and further behind.
I was also behind in book reviews I had committed to, both in the
reading and in the writing. My new novel would be coming out
in about a month, and I was a mess. And then there was the usual
stuff: the grind of a merciless schedule, trying to balance family and
work and writing with too few hours in the day, all with too little
money in the bank and too many bills outstanding.

A gnawing sadness and sense of desperation clung to me as I
worked on the morning's writing, as I got ready for work, as I left
the house.

And then it got worse.

It was raining. Not a hard rain, more of a heavy mist, with a
strong enough wind that an umbrella would have been no use. Not
that I could find mine.

There was something appropriate about standing at the bus
shelter, cold and getting wetter by the minute. They call it pathetic

---

1. Unless otherwise noted, all lyrics quoted in this book were written by Bruce
Springsteen. These, however, were composed by The Hold Steady.

fallacy when an artist uses the external conditions of the world to comment on a character's inner state; when it happens in real life, it just feels... right. I was miserable, and everything was conspiring to keep me that way.

Well, almost everything.

One thing you should know about me, right off the top, is that music is absolutely central to my life. I'm almost always plugged in. I've got a stereo at home and one down at the rented office space where I spend most of my time. I've got a stereo in my office at the bookstore and about 400 CDs there; the bulk of my collection—probably 2,500 CDs—is at the Treasury. I've always got music playing.

Especially on my commute.

So that morning, mired in funk (and not the good James Brown/ Parliament/George Clinton kind), I was plugged in. And over the course of the bus trip, things started to get a little better. An old Tori Amos song came up on the rotation, and I smiled. Lissie's cover of Kid Cudi's "Pursuit of Happiness" perked me up.[2]

And then, as I'm getting off the bus... here come the drums.

Literally.

I had never heard of the Rogue Traders before watching *Doctor Who*'s third-season finale. I still don't know much about them, except that they're an Australian band.

But I broke out into a huge grin. I did a little shuffle-bop across the sidewalk. The rain stopped, and the clouds parted,[3] and the world was right again.

Why?

It was "Voodoo Child." The song itself is a catchy, hooky little number, percussive and danceable.[4] But the boppiness of the song alone wasn't the main reason my day turned.

---

2. I also managed not to sing along, which, given the song's refrain, likely would have gotten me thrown off the bus.

3. That, for the record, is pathetic fallacy.

4. Danceability isn't, as a rule, a crucial thing for me when it comes to music. With the exception of two songs, I don't really dance.

I started renting my office space, a basement suite down the street from our house, a couple of years ago. My wife, Cori, and son, Xander, began referring to it as the Treasury.[5] Most weekend mornings, Xander comes down to the Treasury to hang with me while we give Cori a few hours to sleep in. It's one of my favorite parts of the week. It's our time, his and mine. I'm supposed to be writing, but we end up hanging out, watching TV shows on DVD. We've gone through *Buffy the Vampire Slayer* and *Angel: The Series* several times each. *The Big Bang Theory* and *How I Met Your Mother*.

And *Doctor Who*.

Our second or third time through that show's latest series, Xander developed a fondness for a song that played in the season-three finale: the Rogue Traders' "Voodoo Child," with its refrain of "Here come the drums, here come the drums."[6] It comes at a big moment in the show, and he started to sing along, then asked if we could find it on YouTube. Which we did.

He fell in love with it.

Ten years old, and my son was falling in love with music through a song from a semi-cheesy British sci-fi TV show.[7]

Whenever I hear that song, I can't help but think of Xander, those weekend mornings hanging out with him, that look of sheer joy he had on his face when he listened to the song for the first time.[8]

How can that not make me smile? How can that not bring *me* joy?

That's what music does for me.

---

5. They swear it's not the case, but I suspect an ironic tone nonetheless.
6. The song is composed by James Ash, Elvis Costello, and Steve Davis.
7. In fairness, we've been indoctrinating Xander into music from the time he was wee. He's been attending Broadway shows—on Broadway—since he was three. He can sing whole books—RENT, *Next to Normal*—and judge one performance against another. But this was the first music he had discovered himself. There's a difference.
8. As I go over these pages with a red pen, I'm sitting outside Xander's weekly tap-dancing class. He and his instructor, Alyssa, are working up a routine for the spring recital, set, naturally enough, to "Voodoo Child." And significance layers over significance.

THIS BOOK is about the way certain songs accrete meaning for me, layer upon layer, like how a pearl forms. In particular, it's about the songs of Bruce Springsteen, songs that have acquired the power, the resonance, to stop me in my tracks.

But before I go any further, I have to get a bit of housekeeping out of the way: Mom, Dad? You were right.

It's a painful moment when an almost middle-aged man has to admit that, in print.

I don't know whether it was my mother or my father—or both— who informed me, when I was at a highly resistant age, that there's a fine line between foolishness and idiocy. I've spent the intervening three decades or so demonstrating the validity of their point. I've done some foolish things, and I've been an idiot.

This book manages to straddle that fine line nicely.

It's foolish, on the face of it, to even consider writing about Bruce Springsteen. He's perhaps the most written-about figure in contemporary music, neck and neck with Bob Dylan. Every stone, it seems, has been turned. You can't write a biography (although I've included a short one here, for context), straight music criticism, lyric analysis, political or social perspective: they've all been done before. Hell, even the subject of Springsteen's fans has been done to death.

And then there's the idiocy factor. No one is sure who said it first (I lean toward Charles Mingus or Frank Zappa), but it's been said that writing about music is like dancing about architecture. It's a clever phrase, with a Zenlike clarity. And you don't realize just how true it is until you try to describe a song. You can pile on the metaphors, you can distil things down to fundamentals, you can apply theory, but the song always eludes your grasp.

Given that, why bother trying?

Well, there are two reasons.[9]

---

9. There are a bunch of reasons, actually: I was asked to write this book; I viewed it as a challenge; I like to keep busy, etc., etc. But the two reasons above are the important ones. Let's go with it, okay?

First, because it's Bruce Springsteen. Plain and simple. Springsteen and his music have been a touchstone in my life—literal, emotional, and psychological—for more than twenty-five years now, and aside from a few newsgroup posts and a couple of record reviews, I've never written about him.

The second reason gets to the heart of things, and it goes some distance in obviating both the foolish and the idiotic aspects of this whole endeavor. The second reason has to do with songs, and their significance in our lives.

All of us have songs that touch our souls. Everyone. Even if it's the national anthem at a hockey game, or the song played at your father's funeral, there will be a song that affects you somehow.

That individual response to a song, that resonance, is at the root, I think, of the power of music.

It's a delicate balance, recognizing those individual responses, and writing about my own. Because let's face facts: I'm nothing special. I've written a few books that some readers liked, and I know some cool people, but when it comes right down to it I'm as ordinary as it gets: a smalltown kid living in a small city, a guy with a job and a wife and a son. Hell, we own a minivan.[10] I'm not famous, I'm not in recovery, I'm not bouncing back from a scandal, and I haven't triumphed over crippling odds. I'm just a guy with a laptop and a record collection.

And that's the point, really. This book is about me only because it has to be. If you want to read a redemptive tale about a guy who lost a fortune and a career on hookers and blow, this isn't the book for you. That's not my story.

These are my stories.[11]

---

10. I don't drive said minivan, though. I don't drive at all. Never have. Take a moment to allow that irony to sink in: a guy who doesn't drive writing about Bruce Springsteen, who has an almost fetishistic interest in cars.

11. This is as good a time as any to emphasize a key point: these are *my* stories, from my perspective, and subject to the ravages of time and memory. The people who experienced these events with me might have different recollections, or attach different significance.

And they revolve, in some way or another, around the music of Bruce Springsteen.

I've been a Springsteen fan since I was barely a teenager. By most people's definition, I'm a fanatic: following tours through the Pacific Northwest to see multiple nights of shows in a row, standing in line all day in the pouring rain or the baking sun to get close to the stage, watching setlists develop in real time via the internet, ordering bootlegs from shady vendors in Italy, that sort of thing.[12]

It's deeper than fandom, though. I've grown up with Springsteen as the soundtrack to my life. From my often painful childhood and youth in Agassiz, British Columbia, dreaming of escape, to finally getting out of town, falling in love, becoming a husband, becoming a father, finding a place in the world, the music of Bruce Springsteen has been there.

And I've decided the best way to demonstrate what those songs mean to me is by putting together a mix-tape.

I know that dates me, in this age of CDRs and iPod playlists. The term "mix-tape" is a bit of an anachronism, but the spirit behind it isn't.[13] How many teenagers have attempted to woo the boy or girl of their dreams with a carefully composed mix-tape, using somebody else's words when they were too afraid to use their own? How many road trips have had their own personalized soundtracks? How many hours have been spent in darkened bedrooms, surrounded by albums and scraps of paper, making notes and getting

---

12. Of course, to a lot of folks, I barely register as a fan at all. I know people who have gone to hundreds of shows, who have flown across the country for an acoustic benefit performance, who have followed a Springsteen tour through Europe. I would like to say, as most people would, that those people are nuts. I can't, though: I envy them. Hell, I know people who were at Winterland in 1978! How can you not envy them?

13. Yes, the spirit remains: kids—and adults—are still compiling sets of songs to send messages, as they have since the invention of recordable media. Kids these days, though? They'll never have to include the length of a tape side as a factor in their song selection. They'll never have to do tape math, never have to worry about forgetting to include the length of the cleaner lead. They'll never have to worry about synching a turntable and a tape deck. Kids these days, they've got it so easy. Why, when I was young...

the flow of the music absolutely perfect, balancing the highs and the lows before committing the results to tape?

The mix-tape is a means of communication, a code at times so intricate its true intentions might never be known.

Mix-tapes can also serve as repositories of personal meaning. Writer-director Cameron Crowe[14] apparently has a closet full of aging mix-tapes. Every few months he'd compile what he'd been listening to lately, writing the date on each tape case. Thus, each collection is a snapshot of a moment in time, not only of the music, but of the meaning, a glimpse—like a fading journal—of the past. Mix-tapes such as these are touchstones, repositories of memory and experience, with each listening drawing forth events and emotions with Proustian clarity.

A month or so ago, Peter and I found one of my old mix-tapes in his mom's car.[15] We figured out, eventually, that I'd made it for him twelve or thirteen years before. Playing it was like opening a door, stepping back into our earlier lives.

That's what writing this book has been like: opening a door into the past. And I've had to resist the almost overwhelming temptation to slam it shut again as quickly as I can, because along with the good memories, there are ghosts behind that door, things I've spent a lot of years running from.

We can't control what meaning attaches itself to songs, and sometimes the feelings elicited by a piece of music aren't the sort to make the clouds part and the rain go away. That's all right, though. Any mix-tape is gonna rise and fall. They're like life that way.

---

14. Crowe started out as a teenage rock journalist in the early seventies before becoming a film writer and director. The man has forgotten more about music than most people will ever know, and it shows in his work, from the breathtaking John-Cusack-with-a-boom-box-over-his-head scene in *Say Anything* to the whole of the autobiographical *Almost Famous*, easily the best film ever made about what it means to love rock and roll. For the record? I want to be Cameron Crowe when I grow up.

15. You'll meet Peter in a bit. He's my oldest, dearest friend, and he's lived in Toronto for the last twelve years or so, which, frankly, is way too damn far away.

So here's how this book works. I'm going to start with a brief biography of Springsteen himself. Nothing too in-depth, but enough to get everyone on the same page as to where he comes from and what's happened to him along the way. Bruce 101, if you will.

And then we'll get to the meat of the thing: *Walk Like a Man*. A mix-tape. Liner notes by yours truly.

Just to be clear, in no way is this intended as a generic "greatest hits" package. It's not just a collection of my favorite Springsteen songs either. "Incident on 57th Street," for example, is easily in my top five songs from the man. But it's not here because it doesn't resonate for me the way "My Hometown," a song I don't particularly care for, does. The version of "Born to Run" here isn't the anthem most people would recognize, and "Dancing in the Dark" appears in a later, guitar-driven live version rather than the familiar, synth-heavy top ten hit from 1984. There are also a handful of lesser-known songs, including "Living Proof" and "Thundercrack," that are among the most meaningful of Springsteen's oeuvre, for me.

I've added enough information about each song to allow you to make a copy of *Walk Like a Man* for yourself. I hope you do. I hope you load the songs onto your MP3 player and have them playing as you read. And I hope my stories add a little something to your own.

Three-Minute Records[1]

A BASIC DISCOGRAPHY[2]

Greetings from Asbury Park, N.J. (1973)
The Wild, the Innocent & the E Street Shuffle (1973)
Born to Run (1975)
Darkness on the Edge of Town (1978)
The River (1980)
Nebraska (1982)
Born in the U.S.A. (1984)
Live 1975–85 (1986)
Tunnel of Love (1987)
Chimes of Freedom (EP; 1988)
Human Touch (1992)
Lucky Town (1992)
In Concert: MTV Plugged (1993; DVD released 2004)
Greatest Hits (1995)
The Ghost of Tom Joad (1995)
Blood Brothers (EP; 1996; DVD released 2001)
Tracks (1998)
18 Tracks (1999)

---

1. I have a special spot in my heart for the opening lines of "No Surrender," especially "We learned more from a three-minute record than we ever learned in school." No disrespect to my teachers, but it rings true to me. And yes, I know that "three-minute records" technically refers to singles, but it seemed like a perfect title for a discography.
2. As "basic" might indicate, this isn't an exhaustive discography. I've purposefully ignored singles, twelve-inchers, repackagings, and the like. If you're looking for that sort of a resource, lists are available online. (See Sources.)

The Complete Video Anthology 1978–2000 (DVD; 2001)
Live in New York City (CD/DVD; 2001)
The Rising (2002)
The Essential Bruce Springsteen (2003)
Live in Barcelona (DVD; 2003)
Devils & Dust (2005)
VH1 Storytellers (DVD; 2005)
Born to Run: 30th Anniversary 3 Disc Set (2005)
Hammersmith Odeon London '75 (2006)
We Shall Overcome: The Seeger Sessions (2006)
Live in Dublin (CD/DVD; 2007)
Magic (2007)
Working on a Dream (2009)
London Calling: Live in Hyde Park (DVD/Blu-ray; 2010)
The Promise: The Darkness on the Edge of Town Story (2010)

Growin' Up
A SHORT LIFE OF
BRUCE SPRINGSTEEN[1]

B RUCE FREDERICK SPRINGSTEEN was born September 23, 1949, in Long Branch, New Jersey, the oldest child and only son of parents Douglas and Adele (née Zerilli). They had two daughters as well, Virginia (Ginny) and Pam.

Adele was a legal secretary, and Douglas worked a long series of short-term jobs, including stints at a rug mill, at the county jail, and as a bus driver. The Springsteens weren't poor, exactly, but they maintained a bare-minimum level of financial stability when they weren't downwardly mobile. They lived in Freehold, N.J., an ethnically mixed, working-class town. It was a life of austerity, with Adele making regular visits to the loan company. When things got too dire—such as when the family was evicted—they would temporarily move in with Bruce Springsteen's Italian grandparents.

From his mother and her family, Springsteen got not only his religious faith—the Zerillis were devout Catholics, and Adele never missed Mass—but also openness, compassion, and an early love of music,[2] country and western in particular.

---

1. For the record, there is no such thing as a "straight" biography—such a thing would be a bullet-point list of names and dates without any context whatsoever. Every biography has a point of view, and an agenda, and I'm going to be clear about mine right off the top: this overview of Springsteen's life is going to attempt to locate, in the details of the man's life and world, the roots of elements that run throughout his work, while also giving the reader unfamiliar with Springsteen's background enough context to make the following pages coherent, at the very least.
2. "Pony Boy," the closing track on 1992's *Human Touch*, was a reworking of a traditional lullaby his grandmother used to sing him.

Springsteen's relationship with his father was very different. Where his mother was warm and kindly, his father was cold and forbidding. It wasn't just that Douglas struggled to provide for his family and was prone to drinking; he had an active animosity for his son. "When I was growing up," Springsteen has said in concert, "there were two things that were unpopular in my house. One was me, and the other was my guitar."[3]

Things weren't any better at school. His peers at St. Rose of Lima elementary school ostracized him, both for his poverty and for a social awkwardness that made him seem odd and aloof. His teachers, the nuns, were worse, and his education reads like a surreal litany of mistreatment: as recounted in *Point Blank*, Christopher Sandford's 2000 biography, for example, Springsteen has told of how one sister stuffed him into a garbage can under her desk, "because, she said, that's where I belong." His experiences at school with the sisters, the day-to-day exemplars of his faith, contributed greatly to the lifelong conflict with Catholicism reflected in Springsteen's music, the pull of the religious imagery and beliefs, as opposed to his scorn of its hypocrises and his refutation of its teachings.

Problems at home and confirmed status as a brutalized outsider at school: these could have been the crucial ingredients in the making of a juvenile delinquent. In 1958, though, Springsteen was saved, and I use the word with its the full religious connotation. "I remember when I was nine and I was sittin' in front of the TV and my mother had Ed Sullivan on and on came Elvis," Springsteen is quoted as saying in Sandford's biography. "I remember right from that time, I looked at her and I said, 'I wanna be just... like... that.'"

Adele bought her nine-year-old son his first guitar and paid for lessons. They didn't really take—Springsteen's hands were too small for proper chording, and he was frustrated by rote practice. Four years later, she repeated the gift, this time giving him a yellow Fender from a pawnshop. Springsteen had found his calling.

---

3. The Roxy, Los Angeles, July 7, 1978, as released on *Live 1975–85*.

Freehold Regional High School was as rough on the shy, socially awkward Springsteen as St. Rose of Lima had been. "Basically, I was pretty ostracized in my hometown," Springsteen recalled in a 1995 interview for The Advocate. "Me and a few other guys were the town freaks—and there were many occasions when we were dodging getting beaten up ourselves." At home, his parents were at odds, and Springsteen was often the subject of their arguments. He made jokes about this later in his songs and monologues, but it can't have been easy being the subject of so much support, at times stifling, from his mother and such scorn, from his father.[4] When Springsteen was involved in a motorcycle accident, for example, Douglas sent a barber to cut his son's hair while he was recuperating in hospital and powerless to resist.

Springsteen disappeared into music, spending hours every day practicing his guitar, conditioning himself to play note-perfect versions of the songs spilling out of the radio. "Until I realized that rock was my connection, I felt like I was dying … and I didn't really know why." Sandford writes of Springsteen going further, in the introduction to his 1998 public reading of "We Wear This Mask" by poet Paul Dunbar, when he said, "This is a poem about not feeling free to be yourself. It's about the pain of not being accepted. When I was young, I felt like I needed a mask to be accepted … I was a zero."

---

4. One of the classic "bits" about his parents was recorded at the Roxy in L.A., July 7, 1978, and included in the Live 1975–85 box set. Late in "Growin' Up"—one of the vaguely autobiographical songs from his first album—Springsteen drops into a monologue. "I think—I ain't sure, but I think my mother and father and my sister, they're here again tonight … For six years they've been following me around California, trying to get me to come back home. Hey Ma, give it up, huh? Gimme a break! … They're still tryin' to get me to go back to college. Everytime I come in the house. 'You know, it's not too late, you can still go back to college,' they tell me … My father always said 'You know, you should be a lawyer, get a little something for yourself, you know,' and my mother, she used to say, 'No, no, no, he should be an author, he should write books. That's a good life, you can get a little something for yourself.' But what they didn't understand was, was that I wanted everything. And so, you guys, one of you wanted a lawyer and the other one wanted an author, well, tonight, youse are both just gonna have to settle for rock and roll."

That imagery, of using a mask to move through the world, of multiple faces, surfaces often in Springsteen's work.

In the mid-sixties, Springsteen joined The Castiles, a garage band loosely managed by Tex Vinyard. The band played the local small gig circuit, cranking out covers of the Motown and British Invasion songs that would appear in Springsteen's sets for the next four decades. It wasn't the big time, but Springsteen was a musician, and he discovered one of the fundamental truths of the second half of the twentieth century: chicks dig a guy in a band.

After graduating, barely, from Freehold High in 1967, Springsteen was declared 4-F—ineligible to serve—and thus managed to avoid being sent to Vietnam.[5] He dropped out of community college in 1968 to focus exclusively on his music. He was a key member of several bands in those years, including Earth, a guitar-centered power trio in the Clapton-Cream, proto-heavy-metal mode. It was during this time that he earned the nickname "The Boss," since he—usually sober and not stoned—made sure the band got paid at the end of the night and distributed the earnings.[6]

His family moved to California in 1969, leaving Springsteen to find his own way in the world. He took up residence above a surfboard factory in Asbury Park, a fading vacation town on the Jersey Shore, spending summer days sleeping on the beach and nights on stage in the bars. He became something of a local hero

---

5. How Springsteen avoided the draft is the subject of much discussion, and it forms the subject of one of Springsteen's most haunting monologues, the introduction to "The River" on the Live 1975–85 box set. He talks, in a heartbroken voice, about the constant struggle with his father, who'd often said, "I can't wait till the army gets you... When the army gets you, they're gonna make a man out of you." The story builds in intensity, covering Springsteen's fear of attending his draft physical, and his eventual failure to be accepted, then coming home and telling his father. "My dad said 'Where you been?' I said, 'I went to take my physical.' And he said, 'What happened?' I said, 'They didn't take me.' And he said, 'That's good.'"

6. Godless pinko commie union-boosting bastard that he is, Springsteen isn't fond of the nickname. I'm not either, and I think this is the only point in this book I use it, save for as ironic effect.

during this time, a guitar slinger well known on the Jersey Shore scene. Attempts to break out nationally, however, were less successful. Steel Mill, a Springsteen-led band that featured the talents of, among others, Vini Lopez, Steven Van Zandt, and Danny Federici, received good reviews during a short tour of California and auditioned for legendary rock impresario Bill Graham in 1970, but nothing came of it. Springsteen broke up the band shortly thereafter.

After the deliberate excessiveness of his next band, Dr. Zoom and the Sonic Boom, Springsteen got serious with The Bruce Springsteen Band, a proto–E Street Band with a horn section and female back-up singers, which caught the attention of Mike Appel in late 1971.

Appel was a scrapper, a former songwriter, and low-level music manager. He'd been alerted to Springsteen by Carl "Tinker" West, who managed Steel Mill and The Bruce Springsteen Band. Springsteen flopped in his first audition for Appel, who advised him to write more of his own material. Less than a year later, Springsteen auditioned again. This time Appel agreed to manage the singer, and Springsteen signed management, publishing, and production contracts with him. They would prove to be among the most problematic signatures of his career.

Mike Appel doesn't usually come off too well in the Bruce Springsteen story, but you can't deny the effect the outlandish and usually offensive manager had on the singer's development. Springsteen owes perhaps the most significant moment in his career entirely to Appel: an audition for the legendary John Hammond at Columbia Records in early 1972. Hammond signed Springsteen, and he's been on the Columbia roster ever since.

Although Springsteen was signed as a solo artist, he recruited former bandmates and Jersey Shore hotshots to back him on the record and on tour. With "Miami Steve" Van Zandt on guitar, Gary Tallent on bass, David Sancious and Danny Federici on keyboards, "Mad Dog" Vini Lopez on drums, and Clarence Clemons on saxophone, he created the first iteration of The E Street Band, though it wasn't referred to as such for almost a year.

Greetings from Asbury Park, N.J., was recorded at 914 Sound Studios in Blauvelt, New York, over the summer of 1972. The studio was a leaky, low-fi, antiquated shithole, and the record suffered as a result. The sound of *Greetings* is thin and tinny, the band barely noticeable. Despite significant record company hype and generally positive reviews, the record was a non-starter, selling only eleven thousand copies in the U.S. in its first year.

Springsteen toured incessantly, however, building up a following the old-fashioned way: one audience a night, one new fan at a time.

The band returned to problematic 914 Sound Studios in the summer of 1973, and Springsteen's second album, *The Wild, the Innocent & the E Street Shuffle,* was released in early September.

Despite including such powerhouses as"Rosalita (Come Out Tonight)," "Kitty's Back," and "4th of July, Asbury Park (Sandy)," the more mature, more complex second album fared even more poorly than the debut. Sales were meager, but critics were rhapsodic. Springsteen and the band stayed on the road, night after night, working their magic one venue at a time.

Rock writer and manager Jon Landau was in the audience for the late show at the Harvard Square Theater in Cambridge, Massachusetts, in May 1974. Shortly thereafter, he wrote an epochal, exultant review of the show for Harvard's *The Real Paper* that included these key lines: "I saw rock'n'roll past flash before my eyes. And I saw something else: I saw rock and roll future and its name is Bruce Springsteen."

"Growing Young with Rock and Roll" was a brilliant piece of music writing, melancholy and breathless. Springsteen invited the twenty-seven-year-old Landau (who had, according to Sandford, commented of *Wild & Innocent,* "Loved the album. Not the production.") into the fold.

Springsteen needed help.

Following the dismal sales of his first two albums, Springsteen was in a do-or-die position with his third: if it too failed, his Columbia contract would be little more than paper. He had spent months fumbling with the first single, alternating hours at 914 Sound Studios with nights of performing. The song was "Born to Run," and it was finished only with Landau's assistance.

Work on the remainder of the *Born to Run* album moved relatively quickly, and it was released in the summer of 1975 to waves of hype, engineered by Appel and loathed by Springsteen. The record, which included instant classic songs like the title track, "Jungleland," and "Thunder Road," exploded into the public awareness.

Despite his mixed feelings about fame and hype, by the end of the tour in late 1975 —which took the band overseas for the first time—Springsteen was a bona fide international star. Any sense that he could now take it easy, however, was scuttled by a series of lawsuits, which would keep him out of the studio for almost two years and had the potential to cripple his burgeoning career.

Mike Appel and Jon Landau were never close, and their work together on *Born to Run* served to foster a deep resentment if not an outright hatred between the two men. When Springsteen expressed interest in making Landau part of the team permanently, Appel balked, and Springsteen went back to his contracts to see if he had any leverage. Consultation with Landau and the record company verified his gut feeling: he was being screwed. Springsteen sued Appel to be released from the onerous contracts he had naively signed (which, among other things, saw him receiving a pittance of his earnings and owning none of his songwriting rights), and Appel responded by countersuing to keep Landau and Springsteen out of the studio. "It wasn't a lawsuit about money," Springsteen says in the documentary *The Promise*. "It was a lawsuit about control. Who was going to be in control of my work, and my work life. Early on, I decided that was going to be me."

It was ugly, and got uglier still.

While the lawyers worked, Springsteen split his time between touring and woodshedding with the band at his farm in Holmdel, New Jersey. The shows on the 1976 and 1977 tours are wonders of looseness and spontaneity, with the band roadtesting material they had worked up during the long sessions at Casa Springsteen.[7] Among the songs written and performed during that period[8] was "The Promise," a spiritual successor and counterpoint to *Born to Run*'s "Thunder Road," which many believe to have been written about the lawsuit and Springsteen's relationship with Appel. Springsteen denies that to this day,[9] but "The Promise" remains one of his greatest songs.

It was a brutal, psychologically damaging time, but when the dust settled in 1977, Springsteen had regained control of his songwriting and his career, and Landau stepped in as both producer and manager. The changes didn't end there, however.

Springsteen's fourth studio album, *Darkness on the Edge of Town*, is, as the title suggests, a dark album, graced with moments of hard redemption and faint hopes—a far cry from the passionate urgency of *Born to Run*. In the notes accompanying *The Promise: The Darkness on the Edge of Town Story* in 2010, Springsteen wrote, "'Darkness' was my 'samurai' record, stripped to the frame and ready to rumble."

Live, the songs did indeed rumble. The 1978 tour showed Springsteen at his peak as a performing artist in the E Street Band mode. Shows ran between three and four hours and left audiences in dizzy heaps by their conclusion. On stage, Springsteen was a dynamo: definitely a polished showman, but able to dig deep for emotional truth, night after night.[10] The shows were wild explosions of energy

---

7. *The Promise*, the 2010 film by Thom Zimny that opened at the Toronto Film Festival before being included on *The Promise: The Darkness on the Edge of Town Story*, documents this period of Springsteen's career with disarming clarity and candor. It's well worth watching, even for just the grainy footage of a shirtless Springsteen in his living room leading the band through songs that would later appear on *Darkness on the Edge of Town*.

8. Springsteen wrote and recorded more than seventy songs during the *Darkness* sessions, with a mere ten appearing on the album.

9. In excusing the absence of "The Promise" from the album, Springsteen says, simply, that he was "too close" to it.

10. Nowhere is this more plain than in "Backstreets," which, most nights, broke off in the middle for an extended monologue, part story, part genesis of a new song, "Drive All Night," which would appear on *The River* two years later. That interlude, referred to by fans as "Sad Eyes," was transcendent, show after show: it feels like it's coming straight from the man's soul, and the mere thought of it brings a tear to my eye.

and intensity. "There was a ferocity in the band," recalls E Street Band drummer Max Weinberg in the documentary *The Promise*. "when we finally went out and started playing again, that perhaps wasn't there earlier. It was just an absolutely take no prisoners approach." The tour, which crisscrossed the United States before wrapping late in December 1978, was a triumph, and Springsteen was recognized as part of the mainstream rock pantheon.

Late in the summer of 1979, a few months into the recording sessions for *The River*, Springsteen was invited to headline two nights of the No Nukes concert series at Madison Square Garden in New York, organized in response to the Three Mile Island disaster. It was an opportunity to premiere the title song "The River,"[11] and for Springsteen to embrace his nascent activism.

The River, which was released the following year, was a sprawling two-record set that balanced the existential dread of *Darkness on the Edge of Town* with seemingly throwaway frat-rock songs. Songs like "Independence Day" (perhaps the apotheosis of Springsteen's writing about his father, and something of a rapprochement between the two men), "Point Blank," "Wreck on the Highway," and "Drive All Night" were unremittingly sad, while the title song, a tale of teenage love and adult consequences, is Springsteen near his most existential.

Critics loved *The River*, and it graced many albums of the year lists. Fans snapped it up, and the seemingly constant radio play of the lead single "Hungry Heart" (perhaps the most popular song about a deadbeat dad ever) gained Springsteen even more adherents. It also made tickets a lot harder to come by.

The tour for *The River* was highlighted, in 1981, by Springsteen's first return to Europe since 1975. And in the U.S., the bigger halls and multi-night stands at such venerable venues as Madison Square Garden could have sold out several times over.

---

11. Springsteen introduced the song by saying, haltingly, "This is a song…this is called 'The River.' This is new. This is for my brother-in-law, and my sister." The song was written for and inspired by his younger sister Ginny, who got pregnant when she was seventeen, as the female character does in the song.

The Springsteen story, to this point, is all about incremental increases—publicly, his career kept growing and his social awareness kept deepening. After the conclusion of the tour for *The River*, though, Springsteen's world seemed to shrink.

On a personal level, Springsteen's life had been characterized until then by medium-term relationships and casual liaisons. By Christmas of 1981, though, Springsteen was on his own. He had spent the three months since the end of the tour reading, watching movies, and writing new songs.

Shortly after the turn of the year, Springsteen sat down in his bedroom with a tape recorder, a primitive mixing board, his guitar, and harmonica, and recorded a set of new songs—intended as demos for his next album—in a matter of hours. Those bedroom tracks were released the following September as *Nebraska*.

The album is darkness incarnate, story-songs with elements of autobiography, overwhelming desperation, and fleeting, crumbling redemption. Today, *Nebraska* is widely praised as one of Springsteen's finest works, and is a fixture on most critics' lists of the best albums of all time. It certainly bears the hallmarks of his immersion in the world of American folk music, which was kick-started by his reading of Joe Klein's biography of Woody Guthrie, and of his reading of Howard Zinn's *A People's History of the United States*.

Rather than touring, Springsteen spent more than two years, on and off, in the studio with the band, and hopping on stage at Jersey Shore bars to join up-and-coming acts, usually late in their sets. He became a fixture on the bar scene of his youth, to the point that a surprise appearance became, well, less than surprising.

The recording sessions for the new album proceeded slowly but steadily, and with no small amount of turmoil for Springsteen himself. Part of the difficulty may have been due to Miami Steve Van Zandt announcing that he would be leaving the group upon the album's release to pursue a solo career. Nevertheless, by the time the sessions were finished, in the spring of 1984, Springsteen and the band had created, consciously and deliberately, a sleek, of-the-times hit machine, designed for maximum impact. With former Neil Young guitar slinger and solo artist Nils Lofgren brought in to take Van Zandt's place, and the addition of sassy, redheaded Jersey girl Patti Scialfa on background vocals, The E Street Band was ready to take on the world.

On the heels of its first single, "Dancing in the Dark," the *Born in the U.S.A.* album exploded into the public consciousness in the summer of 1984. Overnight, Springsteen was a household name. An ambitious world tour sold out stop after stop. Seven of the album's twelve songs were released as singles, and they all charted in the top ten.[12] Propelled by those singles, and driven by videos for five of those tracks, the album ended up selling more than fifteen million copies in the United States, and more than thirty million copies around the world.

It wasn't very far into *Born in the U.S.A.*'s life, however, that Boss-mania transcended the music world and infused the culture at large. It was significant enough that Ronald Reagan tried to co-opt what he perceived as Springsteen's patriotism in his run-up to re-election, while Reagan's opponent Walter Mondale also tried to claim Springsteen's endorsement. Adding to the effect was the sudden presence of Springsteen's supposed heartland values being used everywhere in advertising. (Springsteen refused to licence his music or image for any advertising. Madison Avenue went with sound-alikes and lots of flags.)

The biggest indicator of Springsteen's new role in American culture, though, came in the crazed, frantic lead-up to his wedding in 1985.

Springsteen met model and actress Julianne Phillips backstage at a Los Angeles concert in October of 1984. Within months they had announced their engagement, with a wedding scheduled for

---

12. It is a record matched by only two other albums, Michael Jackson's *Thriller* and Janet Jackson's *Rhythm Nation 1814*.

early May in the bride's hometown, Lake Oswego, just south of Portland, Oregon.

The announcement triggered a press reaction akin to that of a royal wedding. So rigorous (and ridiculous) was the attention, in fact, that the wedding actually took place a day earlier than scheduled. The midnight ceremony was accompanied by fake-outs, unmarked cars, police escorts, and other means of subterfuge.

After the ceremony, the groom went back on the road and the bride went back to work.

The final leg of the *Born in the U.S.A.* tour was a stadium swing through major U.S. markets. Springsteen, who had once balked at playing any venue larger than a bar, was now performing—comfortably—for seventy to eighty thousand fans on any given night. The shows changed in focus, growing bigger to fill the spaces, and inevitably losing much of their subtlety and depth. Yet Springsteen still had an impact. During the last shows of the tour, held in late September and early October at the Los Angeles Coliseum, Springsteen stood center stage to deliver a warning to the youth in attendance, a reminiscence of what it was like growing up with the Vietnam War in the background of his youth, and pronouncing that "in 1985, blind faith in your leaders, or in anything, will get you killed." The band then slammed into a scalding cover of Edwin Starr's mid-sixties hit "War."

When the tour was over, Springsteen returned home to New Jersey with his new wife and a new fortune—which some estimated at over $50 million.

He didn't rest, though. In November, Landau sent him a tape of four live tracks from late in the tour, including "War." Springsteen, who had always balked at the idea of a live album, was won over by the tape, and within weeks planning was underway for what would become the mammoth five-record/three CD set *Live 1975–85*.

When it was released in late 1986, the box set was a huge initial success. Propelled by the live performance video for "War," it was a Christmastime hit, the highest selling box set in music history. It was what the fans had been waiting for—sort of. The tracklist came under fire for obsessive quibbles: too much reliance on 1984 and 1985 material, with only one track—the haunting acoustic "Thunder Road" opener—from 1975. There were glaring omissions and puzzling edits. That being said, the *Live* box set was still a fan's dream come true, finally allowing the audience to take a bit of the action home. It was *the* Christmas release in 1986.

After Christmas, though, the set lost all retail momentum, and quickly disappeared.

Much the same thing was happening to Springsteen's marriage. It didn't take long for the Springsteen-Phillips fairytale to turn into drudgery and rancor. What was happening off stage has never been fully explained,[13] but fans became aware of discontent in the household with the October 1987 release of *Tunnel of Love*.

Tunnel of Love was a departure for Springsteen in many ways. Coming off the bombast of *Born in the U.S.A.* and the *Live* box set, it was a quiet album, focused on the perils and problems of love and intimate relationships. And it occupied an uneasy middle ground between a true solo album and an E Street Band project, drawing on the talents of the band members in isolation.

Rather than a celebration of marriage and domestic bliss, as one might expect from a newlywed, *Tunnel of Love* was instead a hard-eyed look at the difficulties of romance and the lies and betrayals between and within individuals in intimate relationships. If anyone had bet money on the longevity of Springsteen's marriage, by the fall of 1987 they were ready to begin counting their losses.

The upheaval in Springsteen's personal life echoed upheaval in his professional life. The *Tunnel of Love* tour was different from any previous E Street Band outing, with many of the traditional warhorses missing in favor of a setlist geared toward songs examining love and relationships, "Born to Run" recast as a mournful, solo acoustic number, and arrangements based on the inclusion of

---

13. Sandford, in *Springsteen: Point Blank*, argues convincingly for a number of factors at play, including infidelity, neglect, conflicting careers, and others. I'm not going to quibble with his conclusions, so if you're interested, you're best off reading his book.

a new horn section, reducing Clemons's importance to the band's sound. Most significantly, Clemons was no longer Springsteen's main onstage foil. That role was now filled by Patti Scialfa, moved up to the front line, within arm's reach of Springsteen.

The shows were powerful and dramatic, as one might expect, but the lingering memory of the concerts wasn't musical, it was personal. The chemistry between Springsteen and Scialfa was palpable: romantic and sexual and clearly electric. When photographs of Springsteen and Scialfa in flagrante in Italy surfaced that summer, it was clear that Springsteen's marriage was over.

The news that Springsteen had hitched his star to Scialfa was met with mixed feelings by much of Springsteen's fan base: no one likes to be confronted with their hero's feet of clay,[14] but the fact is, most of the fandom—especially the female members—had never really taken to Phillips, and the news that Springsteen had now taken up with a fellow musician, and a Jersey girl to boot, was seen as largely positive. It likely helped matters that one of the most compelling rumors concerning the divorce was that Phillips didn't want to have children, or at least not yet. Recasting Springsteen into the role of would-be family man went some distance to ameliorating, in some people's minds, the hint of unsavoriness around the whole matter.[15]

On the heels of the *Tunnel of Love* tour, Springsteen and the band embarked on a multi-artist tour, called Human Rights Now!, in support of advocacy organization Amnesty International[16] and in celebration of the fortieth anniversary of the United Nations Declaration of Human Rights. The six-week tour that fall took the band around the world, and included stops in eastern Europe, India,

---

14. That's a sweeping generalization, I know, and I'm something of an exception to this rule. I actually prefer my heroes to have feet of clay, human foibles, and skeletons in their closets. I don't take the delight in it that some writers, like Sandford, seem to, but there's something oddly comforting about flaws and weakness.

15. Springsteen, to his credit, denies this.

16. Springsteen announced the tour, and his participation in it, on stage during a global radio broadcast of the *Tunnel* tour date in Stockholm that July, before playing a stunning, moving version of Bob Dylan's "Chimes of Freedom."

and Africa before finishing in South America. More significantly, it brought Springsteen into close contact with fellow performers Sting, Peter Gabriel, Tracy Chapman, and Youssou N'Dour.

After the tour ended in late 1988, Bruce Springsteen, for all intents and purposes, disappeared. Springsteen moved from New Jersey to Los Angeles with new girlfriend Scialfa, and, with a few exceptions, was silent for almost four years.

Those exceptions, those moments of broken silence, were significant, to say the least.

The first came in the fall of 1989, when it was revealed that Springsteen had fired the members of The E Street Band. Springsteen wanted to try new things musically, and to avoid becoming hidebound in the still-imposing wake of the *Born in the U.S.A.* experience; the cosmetic changes of the *Tunnel of Love* tour clearly weren't enough. "You can get to a place where you start to replay the ritual, and nostalgia creeps in," he told *Rolling Stone* magazine in 1992. "I wanted to get to a spot where if people came to the show, there'd be a feeling of like, well, it's not going to be this, it's going to be something else." He called each band member individually to tell them the news. "Initially some people were surprised, some people were not so surprised. I'm sure some people were angry, and other people weren't angry. But as time passed, everything came around to a really nice place."

That idea, of coming around to a "really nice place" might be seen as a theme to Springsteen's lost years of the late eighties and early nineties. Although it wasn't a public matter at the time, Springsteen spent those years deliberately stepping away from the machinery that had grown up around him, off the rock star treadmill, and trying to find peace.

His first year with Patti was, apparently, one of almost constant darkness and pain as Springsteen attempted to deal with both a lifetime of emotional scars and the systems he had put into place to deal with those injuries. "The best thing I did was I got into therapy," he recalled in the 1992 *Rolling Stone* interview. "I crashed into myself and saw a lot of myself as I really was." The man who had created a mask for himself as a teenager in order to survive had never really left it behind. It wasn't that he lived to perform; it was that performing was the only place he felt alive, for good and for ill. "I had locked into what was pretty much a hectic obsession, which gave me enormous focus and energy and fire to burn, because it was coming out of pure fear and self-loathing and self-hatred. I'd get on-stage and it was hard for me to stop. That's why my shows were so long. They weren't long because I had an idea or a plan that they should be that long. I couldn't stop until I felt burnt, period. Thoroughly burnt. It's funny, because the results of the show or the music might have been positive for other people, but there was an element of it that was abusive for me. Basically, it was my drug. And so I started to follow the thread of weaning myself."

In this light, Springsteen's firing of the band and his withdrawal from the music world can be seen not as destructive, but as a positive means of stripping away the edifices he had built around himself. As he said, "now I see that two of the best days of my life were the day I picked up the guitar and the day that I learned how to put it down. Somebody said, 'Man, how did you play for so long?' I said: 'That's the easy part. It's stopping that's hard.'"

After the Amnesty tour, Springsteen put his guitar down. He stopped. By most reports, the first year was one of darkness and self-exploration. The next was one of doting fatherhood—to son Evan James, born in the summer of 1990—and delight in his new relationship. He worked with Scialfa on her own album, but most of his time was spent being a father and being a husband. Looking at his life, and what he has said about it, it's clear that he spent the time of his seclusion addressing his own issues about identity, love, and family. He stripped away at the mask. He became the father that he never had, and gave his children—Evan, and later Jessica Rae and Sam Ryan—the childhood that he lacked.

When Springsteen picked up his guitar again, his songwriting and performing reflected these changes and an increased self-awareness.

The first public indication that something was different came in late 1990. Along with Bonnie Raitt and Jackson Browne, Springsteen performed two benefit concerts at L.A.'s Shrine Auditorium in support of the Christic Institute, a left-wing think tank. The two solo acoustic shows, during which Springsteen performed on guitar and piano, were a revelation, and a signal of where he was at, personally speaking.

The setlists for the shows drew deep from Springsteen's catalogue, and also featured several new songs. Older songs, including "My Father's House," "Brilliant Disguise," "My Hometown," and "Darkness on the Edge of Town," were given a thematic unity by the inclusion of three new songs performed over the two nights.

The first, "Red Headed Woman," was a blatantly carnal paean to the pleasures of one particular redhead, who was watching the song's debut from backstage. It was Springsteen playfully revelling in the joys of the flesh, the simplest, and most intimate, of pleasures. Springsteen as a man, shall we say.[17]

The second new song, which premiered the second night, was "The Wish"; it was the first song Springsteen ever wrote about his mother. It's simple and haunting and beautiful, an account of his mother's buying him his first guitar, of her working to support the family—but, more, of her maternal goodness in opposition to his father's darkness: "If pa's eyes were windows into a world so deadly and true, You couldn't stop me from looking but you kept me from crawlin' through." The song finishes by acknowledging the nature of the gift, this song, and his awareness of how overdue it is:

> Well tonight I'm takin' requests here in the kitchen
> This one's for you, ma, let me come right out and say it
> It's overdue, but baby, if you're looking for a sad song, well I ain't
>   gonna play it.

---

17. It's also the finest rockabilly song about cunnilingus ever written by a global superstar in his forties.

Years later, Springsteen acknowledged, "To sing about your mother, that's usually reserved for country singers and gangsta rappers.[18]

The third new song was a revelation. "Real World"[19] is, in a word, stunning, and these performances of the song are among the strongest of Springsteen's career.[20] An account of spiritual and emotional searching, and of eventual love and acceptance, "Real World" has the force of a gospel number while deliberately eschewing the tropes and symbols of such a song: "Ain't no church bells ringing, ain't no flags unfurled, It's just me and you and the love we're bringing, into the real world." Over the course of the song, Springsteen dismisses his old self-pity, and the "shrine" he built of "fool's gold memory and tears cried" before confessing "I wanna find some answers I wanna ask for some help, I'm tired of running scared." It's breathtaking, and if you wonder what Springsteen was doing in his "missing years," it's all right there, nicely encapsulated in a single song.

In early 1992, after another year of almost complete silence (and more than four years after *Tunnel of Love*), it was announced that Springsteen would release two new albums, simultaneously, that spring.

Human Touch was the result of a lengthy writing and recording process that spanned almost two years (the record included "Real World" and "57 Channels," both performed at the Christic benefits more than a year earlier), and featured the talents of a variety of hired studio players, as well as former E Streeter Professor Roy Bittan.

After working on it for more than a year, Springsteen had apparently shelved the album in mid-1991 (as he had done with several

---

18. From his introduction to "The Wish," November 8, 1996.
19. Composed by Bruce Springsteen and Roy Bittan.
20. I realize I should have considerable moral quandaries about bootleg recordings of Springsteen shows, but performances like the Christic benefits, and the debut of "Real World" in particular, make those questions moot. Quite simply, the world would be a poorer place were there no record of these performances. Yes, they ARE that good.

other projects), but returned to it shortly thereafter, deciding he needed one more song to round it out before release. "Living Proof," the song he wrote to fill that slot, didn't fit, thematically. It felt like a new beginning, and Springsteen treated it as such, writing nine more songs and recording an entire second album, *Lucky Town*, in less than two months. Springsteen elected to release *Human Touch* and *Lucky Town* at the same time, as distinct but complementary halves of an uneasy whole.

Springsteen's instincts were spot on: there is a marked difference in tone and theme between the two albums. *Human Touch*, with songs like the title track and "Real World," highlights the movement from the fear and the difficulties of relationships explored on *Tunnel of Love* toward acceptance and trust. It's a difficult journey, and the album's final track, a hushed, intimate version of "Pony Boy," serves as a grace note—a sign that perhaps, just this once, the journey ends in the safety and comfort of a home and family.

If *Human Touch* is the journey, *Lucky Town* is the destination. The record has its roots in "Living Proof," which begins by chronicling Evan's birth, but also explores the power of the singer's own mind to imprison him, and his escape from his own self-imposed bonds to find a family, "a close band of happy thieves." The album also pokes good-natured fun at Springsteen's fame, celebrates the singer's current happiness, acknowledges the risks of trust, and confirms the faith and confidence he has in the relationship. Yet it's not all hearts and flowers. "Souls of the Departed" is a political anthem rooted in the deaths of soldiers in the Gulf War and a child in Compton.

It's useful to consider *Human Touch* and *Lucky Town* alongside *Tunnel of Love* when measuring of Springsteen's developing inner consciousness. While they are unquestionably the work of the same man, one can see, vividly, the changes worked by and within those five missing years. As Springsteen told *Rolling Stone*, "*Human Touch* was definitely something that I struggled to put together... At the end, I felt like it was good, but it was about me trying to get to a place. It sort of chronicled the post–*Tunnel of Love* period... I'd spent a lot of time writing about my past, real and imagined, in some fashion. But with *Lucky Town*, I felt like that's where I am. This is who I am. This is what I have to say. These are the stories I have to tell. This is what's important in my life right now."

Given that there hadn't been a Springsteen tour since 1988, it was crucial for him to go back on the road. With no E Street Band, Springsteen held auditions, and relied on Bittan's input to assemble a group of young players; Bittan would take on the role of onstage coach, which Van Zandt had held so long in The E Street Band. After much rehearsal and several preview gigs, the new band headed to Europe to open the tour.

Before they left, though, the fate of the two albums was already in motion. They both debuted near the top of the charts, but they didn't linger there long, falling off the top forty almost as soon as they had reached it. In addition to the poor sales, the albums also received something else which Springsteen hadn't faced in several decades: decidedly mixed reviews.

Despite the poor reception accorded the new albums, and the general scorn of the fan community for Springsteen choosing to tour with a new band (especially behind material which would—to their ears—have been a comfortable fit for The E Street Band[21]), the tour was, generally speaking, a commercial success, and included such benchmarks as eleven shows at New Jersey's Meadowlands Arena selling out in little more than two hours.

Early in 1993, Springsteen was approached by director Jonathan Demme about the possibility of his contributing a song to the soundtrack of a film he was making about a lawyer, played by Tom Hanks, who contracts AIDS and sues his firm for wrongful dismissal. *Philadelphia* would go on to become one of the first mainstream film treatments of the disease, and earned Hanks his first Academy Award for Best Actor.

---

21. The band on the world tour of 1992–93 is still referred to by many fans as, simply, "the other band." You have to curl your lip slightly to say it correctly.

Springsteen wrote and recorded his contribution to the soundtrack in the summer of 1993. "Streets of Philadelphia" was a top ten single upon its release in early 1994,[22] and became something of an anthem for the gay community despite the fact that, lyrically, there is nothing in the song even implicitly about AIDS, gay rights, or homophobia. Indeed, it lyrically and thematically resembles some of the sadder songs on *Human Touch*. It is, however, tremendously moving, a plangent prayer set against a heavy rhythm track.

And in March of 1994, it won Bruce Springsteen the Academy Award for Best Original Song (he had won the Golden Globe too, earlier).

Aside from the flurry around "Streets of Philadelphia," and his new role as a Hollywood celebrity, 1994 was a quiet year for Springsteen. He and Scialfa's youngest child, Sam Ryan, was born in January, and Springsteen was largely out of public view.

Rumor has it that Springsteen was suffering from writer's block over the course of 1994, which shines light on his decision, in early 1995, to re-form The E Street Band for a week of studio sessions to record several new songs for a planned *Greatest Hits* album. Three of the four "new" songs released on the album were written years before, although "Secret Garden" was a new work (and had a labored quality one might expect from a writer working his way through a block). The sessions were filmed for a documentary, which is illuminating in that it demonstrates just how conscientious Springsteen was with the image he wanted to present to the world. One would never know, from *Blood Brothers*, the level of anger many of the E Street Band members were still carrying over their sacking. An abbreviated performance with the band at the end of the week at a New York bar provided footage for the video for "Murder Incorporated," and served as a reminder for those in the

---

22. In fact, it is—as of this writing—Springsteen's last top ten single.

audience[23] just how much had been lost when Springsteen parted ways with the E Streeters.

Springsteen apparently didn't see it that way. Following the February release of Greatest Hits,[24] he once again turned his back on The E Street Band and began working on the songs that would be released in the fall as The Ghost of Tom Joad.[25] These songs demonstrate a different approach to songwriting for Springsteen.

Perhaps as a way of circumventing the rumored writer's block, Springsteen begin building his songs based on external influences, rather than internal inspiration. It's a more journalistic approach, with the song "The Ghost of Tom Joad" updating the classic character from John Steinbeck's The Grapes of Wrath[26] into the poverty-stricken, contemporary southwest, while "Balboa Park" and "Sinaloa Cowboys" were drawn from newspaper coverage of illegal Mexican immigrants drawn into child prostitution and the crystal meth trade, respectively.

The Ghost of Tom Joad is seen as the spiritual heir to Nebraska, more than a decade later. Certainly the approach is similar, rooted in acoustic instrumentation, but Joad had very much a deliberate album-making process, lacking the accidental wonder that was Nebraska. It's a comfortable album, its warm textures and rich tonalities at odds with the starkness of its material.

---

23. And those who heard or saw it on bootleg.
24. The Greatest Hits album was neither a commercial nor a critical slam dunk. It was pleasantly, and politely, received, but anyone envisioning a chart-topper was disappointed. Worse still, the new songs were widely regarded as pale in comparison to such classics as "Born to Run," "Atlantic City," and "The River."
25. He made a couple of further concert appearances with the E Street Band, including a filmed gig at Sony Studios, and the opening ceremony concert for the Rock and Roll Hall of Fame in Cleveland. But these had the feeling of obligation rather than passion. Curiously, he also spent almost a month on the road with Joe Grushecky and the Houserockers, playing sets which mixed originals from both men.
26. Reportedly Springsteen, an inveterate movie junkie, was first inspired by John Ford's film of the novel, though he later read the book as well. Journey to Nowhere: The Saga of the New Underclass, by journalist Dale Maharidge and photographer Michael Williamson was another key inspiration.

Also very different from the *Nebraska* experience was that Springsteen chose to tour in support of the album. The *Joad* tour was a staid affair: solo, acoustic shows performed in concert halls and theatres around the world over the period of a year and a half.

The shows mixed new songs from *Joad* with radically re-envisioned versions of some of his classics (including an intense version of "Born in the U.S.A." that clarified once and for all the actual meaning of the song, for anyone still unclear). Springsteen definitely had a vision in mind for the concerts, and it shows in his performance style. For once, he's not loose. He downplays and under-sings at every opportunity, and this, combined with often simplistic arrangements, forces the lyrics into stark relief. These are stories he is telling, and he wants his listeners to focus on every word. To this end, he began almost every show by admonishing the audience not to sing or clap along, and generally to "shut the fuck up."[27] Springsteen, the reluctant student, had become something of a stern teacher.

As the tour progressed, Springsteen gained something that had, thus far in his career, eluded him: credibility. He had long been loved and admired, cheered and fawned over, but in a way, he had never been respected. With the *Joad* tour, Springsteen became the thinking man's rock star, which was perhaps an odd role for a community college dropout. The *Joad* album and tour, with its central literary allusion and its journalistic rootedness, placed him in the American literary continuum in the footsteps of Steinbeck himself.

Springsteen's nomination for a second Academy Award, for "Dead Man Walkin'," the title song to the Sean Penn film about the awakening of anti–death penalty activist Sister Helen Prejean, only added to his credibility.

The tour stop on the night of November 8, 1996, was, in many ways, a typical *Joad* show. All of the elements were the same—a small hall, the twang in Springsteen's voice (which he adopted

---

27. Fans refer to the *Joad* tour as the Shut the Fuck Up Tour.

when he started writing about the American southwest), the often-pinched vocals—and the setlist included most of the usual numbers. What set the show apart was the venue itself.

On the night of November 8, 1996, Bruce Springsteen went home.

The show at St. Rose of Lima school was a benefit for the school and a community center, and it was the first time Springsteen had stood on the stage of his primary school since the mid-sixties when, as a member of The Castiles, he had played covers for youth dances there. This time, he was one of the world's most famous men, a multi-millionaire in his mid-forties who managed to still be the voice of the people; a man who had spent the better part of the last decade coming to terms with his life and his psyche and addressing his demons, many of which could trace their roots back to Freehold, if not to that very school.

In Freehold, with the substitution and addition of a few songs, the basic *Joad* setlist is[28] transformed—to my mind, at least—into something of a summation of Springsteen's life and concerns. In many ways, the performance at St. Rose of Lima brings everything full circle.

Springsteen certainly seems to have been aware of this, even in the moment. That night, Springsteen opened the show with "The River," rather than "The Ghost of Tom Joad." While the familiar opening lines, about growing up in the area, elicited a cheer from the crowd, the song as a whole shifted the meaning of the night: this wasn't going to be an outward-looking show, focusing on the tragedies of others. It was going to be personal.

From the stage of his former parochial school, he sang about his mother and her struggles and her inspiration to him ("The Wish"). In front of a hometown crowd, perhaps including some of the very people who had ostracized him and called him weird, he spoke about how he used to skulk around to avoid getting beaten up. In

---

28. Yes, "is"—I'm listening to the show as I write this, through the miracle of bootlegging.

front of the nuns, the spiritual descendants of the women of God who had tormented him and called him trash, he sang one of the defiant anthems of his youth ("Growin' Up"). In the very place where his faith was shattered, he performed songs drawing on the shards of that faith ("Adam Raised a Cain," "The Promised Land"). He dedicated "This Hard Land" to Marion Vinyard, widow of Tex Vinyard, the manager of The Castiles, who had opened her home to the teenage band.

And over the course of the evening, in the very town where his father grew angry and bitter under the weight of poverty and intermittent work, he sang a number of songs about Douglas, and their relationship. From the stark filial despair of "Adam Raised a Cain" to the simple, touching "Used Cars," from the haunting "Mansion on the Hill" to a conciliatory "My Hometown,"[29] Springsteen put his relationship with his father into the forefront that night.

The show is remarkable to listen to, knowing what we know of Springsteen and his life. It's a low-key and careful performance, every song performed deeply and intently, as if ensuring that none of his meaning is overlooked. Over the course of twenty-four songs, Springsteen takes a look back, and a look out, reconciling himself not only to his past, but to the town itself. It's exorcism by music.

The extent to which this is true is demonstrated by the final song Springsteen performed that night, a new song he said from the stage he would perform only once[30]: "In Freehold."

The song itself is something of a throwaway. It's virtually a spoken folk track, with clunky rhymes and awkward meter, clearly composed for the occasion. It hardly panders, though. In fact, in one song, Springsteen seems to address the concerns of his entire adult life. With a metronomic refrain of "In Freehold," Springsteen talk-sings about his childhood, including how his sister got pregnant as a teen, how the town broke his father, how he learned his love

29. Which drew a deafening roar of approval from the audience.
30. He has performed it since, but it's among the rarer songs in his catalogue.

for music, how he had his first kiss on a Friday night, and his heart broken many times, how it was a redneck town, cruel to those who didn't fit in, and about his education in that very school.

It's one of the keys to therapy: you need someone to listen, someone to whom you can tell your stories. For one night, Springsteen was able to tell his stories to the people in them. He was able to finish the circle, to come home again, not as a conquering hero—though he was certainly treated as one—but as a kid from the neighborhood, grown up and at peace with the course of his life, reconciled to his past, comfortable in the present, and looking to the future.

After he finished the song, Springsteen posed on stage for photos, as he had promised he would. Later that night, he left town, and headed home.

FIFTEEN YEARS later, it's possible to see that night as something of a turning point in Springsteen's career.

The time since has seen an almost unprecedented level of productivity from the singer, and a daring that wasn't there early in his career. What's missing in the years since is the palpable sense of conflict that was so apparent[31] earlier on.

The *Joad* tour continued well into 1997, and after that Springsteen turned himself to a project that surprised many people: combing his vaults and compiling a box set of outtakes and alternate versions. *Tracks*, upon its 1998 release, was something akin to the Holy Grail for fans, something for which they had desperately wished and had largely, given Springsteen's long history of perfectionism, given up on ever seeing.

Tracks was a treasure trove, covering from Springsteen's earliest days as a recording artist (the set begins with John Hammond's voice, from Springsteen's audition tape), through his over-prolific days from 1976 to 1984. A lot of fan bootleg favorites were present

---

31. Well, once you know to look for it.

and accounted for, including "Thundercrack," "Iceman," and the original solo acoustic recording of "Born in the U.S.A.," and a handful of missing B-sides, including "Roulette," "Pink Cadillac," and "Be True." The real revelation, though, were the songs from the *Tunnel of Love* sessions, and almost a disc worth of tracks from the missing years, 1989–93.

The past was clearly on Springsteen's mind through 1998, and for a good, non-musical reason: late in May, his father Douglas died, at age seventy-three. The relationship between the Springsteen men had warmed somewhat, starting in the early 1980s,[32] reaching a final, loving rapprochement around the time of the birth of Bruce's first son. He would visit his parents in California often, and the two men would take off on road trips,[33] driving without a destination, just spending time together. "I feel lucky to have been so close to my dad as I became a man and a father myself," Springsteen said in a carefully worded statement.

This sense of conciliation with and openness to his past extended to his former cohorts. Shortly after he completed the media rounds to promote the *Tracks* set, Springsteen began calling the former members of The E Street Band, asking them if they would be interested in touring. Despite the circumstances of their firing, and some lingering hard feelings, everyone said yes, including Miami Steve Van Zandt, who had left the band in 1984 and was by then appearing on *The Sopranos*. Springsteen also added violinist Soozie Tyrell, who had appeared on *The Ghost of Tom Joad*, to the band.

The reunion tour stretched over 1999 and 2000, and took Springsteen and the reconstituted band around the world yet again.

---

32. This rapprochement had at least as much to do with a shift in the son as it did with any change in the father, which is often the way of these things. A turning point seems to have come, for Bruce, in the late 1970s, around the time he wrote "Independence Day," with its critical line "I guess that we were too much of the same kind."

33. Springsteen credits these trips with increasing his awareness of the problems along the Mexican border, and cites them as one of the influences for the songs on *The Ghost of Tom Joad*.

Unlike previous tours, there was no "new" music to play—instead, the band drew on *Tracks* and the wealth of Springsteen's now sizable catalogue. The shows were, on many levels, stunningly successful. Financially, they were an unparalleled success, selling out almost every night, with Springsteen taking an unprecedentedly high cut from the venues. Musically, they were as powerful as ever, with The E Street Band performing at very near the top of their game every night (though nothing comes close to the 1978 tour in terms of sheer headlong rush). There was, however, something a bit too professional about the shows, especially as the tour continued. It's not that the performances became hidebound, but they began to lack the spontaneity of Springsteen at his best.

Springsteen seemed to have no plans following the conclusion of the reunion tour in July 2001. However, the terrorist attacks on New York and Washington, D.C., on September 11, 2001, galvanized Springsteen into artistic action. He immersed himself in his community, and began writing songs.

Less than a year after the attacks, Springsteen released *The Rising*, the first new album from Bruce Springsteen and the E Street Band in eighteen years. *The Rising* was released on a massive wave of hype, which exceeded in its directness even *Born in the U.S.A.*–mania at its peak, and the album and tour conferred a new status on Springsteen: national healer. The album, which drew from the stories of the victim's families and chronicled acts of faith and heroism, was Springsteen's best-selling album since *Tunnel of Love*, and with the blast of public exposure Springsteen regained whatever position of pre-eminence he had lost in the early 1990s.

The band toured for more than a year.

In 2004, Springsteen entered the political fray, throwing the full force of his celebrity behind presidential candidate John Kerry, who was running against incumbent George W. Bush. Springsteen not only endorsed the Vietnam veteran and protestor turned senator, he and The E Street Band also headlined one of several traveling rock and roll caravans under the banner of the Vote for Change tour.

While the tours were very effective in raising money and aware-ness, they didn't succeed in getting Kerry elected.

Despite this failure, Springsteen's position as a member of the rock and roll aristocracy carried him through the rest of the decade, and allowed him to take substantial artistic risks. When touring behind 2005's largely acoustic *Devils & Dust*, for example, Spring-steen played arenas,[34] rather than the theatres of the *Joad* tour, relying only on his guitar, piano, and talents (and a deep look back into the catalogue for rarities and one-offs) to conquer the at-times cavernous spaces.

Less well-received was his 2006 foray into the world of tra-ditional folk and roots music with *We Shall Overcome: The Seeger Sessions*. Performing with an ad hoc band of local performers, as well as Soozie Tyrell, The Miami Horns, and Patti Scialfa, Springsteen recorded an album's worth of songs affiliated with folk icon and firebrand Pete Seeger, including "Eyes on the Prize," "Shenandoah," "Froggie Went a-Courtin'," and the title track. It's a joyous and enthusiastic album, and was met with considerable critical acclaim upon its release. The public response was much more muted. Not only did the album fail to sell at Springsteen's usual level, but tick-ets for the ensuing tour were readily available, even in traditionally strong Springsteen markets.[35]

Scarcely pausing to take a breath, Bruce Springsteen and the E Street Band released a new album, *Magic*, in October of 2007, less than a year after the conclusion of the *Sessions* tour. The bulk of the songs were written in late 2006, and many reflect a deep unease with the state of American politics and society in the waning years of the Bush administration. Spiritually, *Magic* is close kin to *Darkness*

---

34. This move to arenas for the *Devils & Dust* tour was another of those decisions that some fans saw as sacrificing art on the altar of commerce.

35. Interestingly, the album and tour fared much better in Europe than in the United States. Springsteen actually cut short the projected American tour, and toured Europe twice with The Sessions Band. It's no accident that the official DVD release of the tour was recorded in Dublin and not Duluth.

on the Edge of Town, though sharply topical, with songs like "Gypsy Biker," "Last to Die," and "Long Walk Home" capturing the zeitgeist as cannily as *The Rising* had, though with much less fanfare.

Propelled by the intense lead-off single, "Radio Nowhere" (as close as Springsteen has ever come to writing a punk song), *Magic* returned Springsteen to the charts, and resulted in a run of near-sellout arenas for the ensuing tour.

All was not rosy, however. In November 2007, on the eve of the European tour, Danny Federici was forced to withdraw from the band, unable to travel while seeking treatment for aggressive melanoma; he died in 2008. The band was still on the road, and the shows following Federici's death all opened with a photo tribute to the organist, set to "Blood Brothers," which had become a band theme since the finale of the reunion tour. Springsteen also delivered a eulogy at Federici's funeral, and "The Last Carnival," from 2009's *Working on a Dream*, is a tribute to his fallen friend.[36]

After the conclusion of the *Magic* tour in mid-2008, Springsteen went to work in support of Barack Obama's bid for the presidency. Springsteen played numerous rallies and speeches, and his November 2 appearance featured the debut of the song "Working on a Dream." While the campaign didn't feature anything quite as ambitious as the Vote For Change tour, it met with decidedly better—if you were Springsteen, or a Democrat—results.

In a period of three weeks in January and February 2009, Springsteen had the unique fortune of winning a Golden Globe (for his song "The Wrestler," from the film of the same name), playing at an inaugural celebration for President-elect Obama (on the steps of the Lincoln Memorial), releasing a new album (*Working on a Dream*), and performing the halftime show at the Super Bowl. Not a bad way to start a year that would see another mammoth tour, this time

---

36. The song picks up, stylistically and thematically, from *The Wild, the Innocent & the E Street Shuffle*'s "Wild Billy's Circus Story," which was highlighted by Federici's accordion playing. Springsteen also supported the Danny Federici Melanoma Fund by donating all the proceeds from a digital EP entitled *Magic Tour Highlights*, which included the performance of "4th of July, Asbury Park (Sandy)" from Federici's last concert.

with headlining performances at England's Glastonbury Festival and the Hard Rock Calling concert in London's Hyde Park.

The latter show, which was released on DVD in 2010, shows a performer clearly at ease with himself. Three months before his sixtieth birthday, he jokes about his age while delivering a performance that would humble most younger rockers: twenty-seven songs, stretching more than three hours from the opening cover of The Clash's "London Calling" to a closing "Dancing in the Dark," from the heat of the late afternoon well into the cool of a summer evening. Springsteen left yet another crowd—this one estimated at more than fifty thousand people—utterly sated, hoarse-voiced, and likely barely able to stand.

Just another day at the office for the boy from Freehold. Just another gig. It's what he does; it's what he's always done. From his childhood bedroom in a shotgun house on the wrong side of the tracks, through every two-bit bar in the United States, then into the White House and to Hyde Park, once again, on stage, it's who he is.

"What will he do next?" has long been the great question when it comes to Springsteen. On June 18, 2011, that question took on a sad weight with the death of Clarence Clemons, age sixty-nine, from the aftereffects of a recent stroke. Clemons was widely regarded as the heart and soul of the E Street Band; his death made headlines worldwide.[37]

Springsteen left no doubt as to the depth of his loss. In a statement on brucespringsteen.net, he said, "He was my great friend, my partner, and with Clarence at my side, my band and I were able to tell a story far deeper than those simply contained in our music. His life, his memory, and his love will live on in that story and in our band."

As always, for Bruce Springsteen, it comes down to people, and love, and stories.

---

37. I was alone in a hotel room in Vancouver, reading over the page proofs for this book when I heard the news. I spent the next few hours listening to some of Clemons's greatest moments on my cell phone and communing with fans on Twitter and Facebook. They say a grief shared is a grief halved, but I don't know if that's true.

A MIX-TAPE

WALK LIKE A MAN

Side One

"Rock and roll saved my
life when I was a teenager.
It's still saving it now."
PATTERSON HOOD *of Drive-by Truckers,
live in Seattle, 2008*

Rosalita
(Come Out Tonight)

Album: *The Wild, the Innocent & the E Street Shuffle*
Released: September 11, 1973
Recorded: June–August 1973
Version discussed: Video recorded at the Arizona Veterans
Memorial Coliseum, Phoenix, July 8, 1978 (*Darkness* tour)

ONE OF THE keys to a good mix-tape is to start off strong. And it doesn't get any stronger than this: "Rosalita (Come Out Tonight)" is perhaps *the* Springsteen concert warhorse. For a decade, it was the finale of virtually every show, six to eight minutes of rock and roll defiance and communion, a melodic, exultant cry against the people—his girlfriend's parents, in particular—who didn't believe in the narrator's musical dreams, plus a triumphant whoop at getting the fat advance from the record company, which finally proves his worth. It's difficult not to hear it as a personal song, although the lyrics don't mesh up against what we know of Springsteen's life. That doesn't matter, however: the song rings true, whether it's actually true or not.[1]

For me, "Rosalita" is where it all started.

In the spring of 1984, I was thirteen years old. My parents had separated, and my brothers and I were living with my mom, seeing my dad for dinner once a week and spending every second weekend at the place he shared with Sue, who would later become my stepmother.

---

1. The line between "honest" and "true" is key to Springsteen's work.

One of the great things about my dad's place was that he had a satellite dish. Not one of those demure, dinner-plate-sized numbers you see affixed to urban apartment buildings and houses these days. His dish was a backyard monstrosity, eight feet in diameter. From the looks of it, my dad could have coordinated a nuclear first-strike from his recliner. Instead, we watched movies on HBO, Cinemax and The Movie Channel. We got addicted to professional wrestling and badly dubbed kung fu movies on one of the Atlanta superstations.

And we watched MTV.

To a chubby, glasses-wearing loner and scapegoat like me, growing up in a town of less than four thousand souls with neither a bookstore nor a record store (let alone a movie theatre or mall), those videos were literally a message from the beyond. There was a whole world out there, just out of reach, and it was being beamed into my life in three-and-a-half-minute chunks, twenty-four hours a day.

Let's not overlook one salient fact, though: the early eighties was a shitty, shitty time for music. I've grown to appreciate New Wave and the New Romantics as an adult (I'll even confess to a grudging fondness for Duran Duran, if pressed), but back in the day it was all skinny ties and synthesizers and pretty boys on sailboats. Nary a guitar nor an intelligent lyric in sight. Sure, I liked David Bowie, but he didn't speak to me, at least in his then-contemporary "Let's Dance"/*Serious Moonlight* stage.

That all changed in the spring of 1984.[2]

---

2. The fact that it was the spring of 1984, and not the summer, has, as any Springsteen fan will tell you, a certain significance. After the June release of *Born in the U.S.A.*, the world went Springsteen-crazy. The "Dancing in the Dark" video—with Courtney Cox at her winsome, non-speaking best—went into heavy rotation. Politicians name-checked him left and right, and the tour quickly made the transition from arenas to stadiums. If you "discovered" Springsteen during this time of media saturation, a whiff of bandwagon-jumping sticks to you in certain fan circles even twenty-five years later. Especially if you ever wore a bandanna to a concert, or you now state that "Glory Days" is your favorite Springsteen song. For the record, and just so we're clear: spring of 1984, no bandanna, loathe "Glory Days."

In the run-up to the release of the first single from Springsteen's forthcoming album, MTV pulled out all the stops. I remember constant coverage, a contest (Be a Roadie with Bruce!), and "Rosalita."

There are dozens of fantastic versions of "Rosalita," but for me the definitive version is the grainy video that MTV played incessantly that spring. Filmed in Phoenix, Arizona, on July 8, 1978, during the *Darkness on the Edge of Town* tour, it was a Saul on the road to Damascus revelation for me. You've got to see it to believe it.[3] It is, to my mind, everything rock and roll is, and everything it can be. And really? Everything it should be.

The song starts with a crash, Springsteen slamming into the opening guitar chords, Clarence Clemons's saxophone wailing. The E Street Band is tight, navigating its way through hairpin changes, up-tempo, down-tempo, Springsteen playing his bandmates as surely as he plays his guitar. He stalks the stage, he jumps, he drops, he slides: this is a blood and guts performance, all the more impressive when you realize that there was nothing special about the concert. It was just another gig for Springsteen in the summer of 1978.

What comes across most strongly, however, is Springsteen's unfettered joy: he's entirely in the moment, and the power he brings to the song can barely be contained to the stage or the screen. In the "Rosalita" video, Springsteen is messianic, and a goof, and a true believer, all at the same time. It's almost impossible to look

---

3. I suspect (cough) that it's available online—if you go looking, you want the longer (nine-plus minutes) version, which includes the band introductions cut for the first official video release. The full version—band introductions intact—was released on an *Old Grey Whistle Test* anthology. And, thankfully, in October 2010, Springsteen Inc. finally released the full version of "Rosalita," on one of the DVDs included in the box set *The Promise: The Darkness on the Edge of Town Story.* (It's not that simple, though. The version in the box set was actually recut by director Thom Zimny, who had access to footage from all the cameras. Zimny also managed to correct the sound, though, which was always a little fast, so say what you will about historical revisionism, it does have its advantages.) The box also includes, for the first time, video of an entire *Darkness* tour show (Houston, December 8, 1978). This, for your average Springsteen fan, is roughly the equivalent of finding the Holy Grail on a pallet at the local Costco.

away as he digs into the verses, as he engages in a cross-stage face-off with the Big Man while standing atop Roy Bittan's piano, as he introduces the band. It's mesmerizing, and it makes you glad to be alive.[4]

Throughout the performance, girls dodge security to tackle Springsteen at the microphone stand, to steal kisses. The video ends with him being piled upon by a group of women at the edge of the stage. With the help of security he manages to drag himself away, emerging from a full-on kiss with a dazed, pleased, what-the-fuck-just-happened look that says it all.

Seeing the video as a thirteen-year-old, I felt my brain explode. This wasn't the twee synth profundity of Orchestral Manoeuvres in the Dark, or the mock-operatic aspirations of Iron Maiden: this was honest, and true, and it made me feel. Really feel.

I watched that video as often as I could. MTV operated on a system of repeats every few hours, and when the time came around I would chase my brothers off the TV and take over the living room, turn the stereo up as loud as it would go, and lose myself into total rock-geek bliss. Even when I wasn't watching the video, I couldn't shake the song. I'd catch myself singing the chorus, making up words for the bits I didn't know. I sang myself hoarse on "Rosalita." I remember vividly being sent down to my grandmother's basement to get ice cream for dessert, and her yelling down the stairs, wondering what was taking me so long. I had surrendered to an air-guitar attack, my arms flailing wildly, making all the right rock star moves.

I air-guitared that motherfucker to death that spring.

It was the first Springsteen song that I ever heard,[5] and it was like I had been waiting for it my whole life.[6]

---

4. As Craig Finn of The Hold Steady is wont to say, thirty-odd years later, "There is so... much... joy in what we do." But more on that later.

5. Well, not really. I was an ardent radio listener, and I had of course heard "Hungry Heart," ad nauseam, after 1980. But I didn't identify that song with anyone in particular, let alone Springsteen. To this day, I don't identify it with Springsteen—it's so

Born in the U.S.A. was released a couple of months later. I was primed for it, to say the least. In fact, it's the first record I can remember actively anticipating.

The release of the "Dancing in the Dark" single did give me pause as I waited: the song was so slick, so glossy, so commercial. Where was the grit? Where was that dork messiah shaking himself free of those screaming girls? And what the fuck: was that a *synthesizer?!*

But those fears dissipated in about the time it took to count in the first bars of "Born in the U.S.A." itself. There it was: fire, passion, integrity, grit. I was a goner, and I've never looked back.

> Now I know your mama she don't like me 'cause I play in a rock
>   and roll band
> And I know your daddy he don't dig me but he never did understand

unlike anything else he's ever done, I'm convinced it was actually recorded by anonymous studio musicians and accidentally included on *The River.* Why it became popular, I'll never know. I do know this, though: if I never hear it again, it'll be too soon.

6. As I wrote this, I realized something: my falling in love with "Rosalita" was kind of a set-up. I had actually seen that very video years before! It was included in a movie about the history of rock and roll I saw at my grandmother's place one night. I was more interested in early Elvis and Beatles stuff at that time, but I think that viewing planted the "Rosalita" seed in my head, *Manchurian Candidate* style. When the seed was triggered that spring of 1984, I exploded all to hell.

My Hometown

Album: *Born in the U.S.A.*
Released: June 4, 1984
Recorded: January 1982–March 1984

COMING OFF the bombast and exuberance of a live version of "Rosalita," the transition into "My Hometown" (the studio version, no less) is the musical equivalent of slamming headfirst into a brick wall. That's by design, and it's precisely the feeling I get every time I hear the song.

I don't actively dislike "My Hometown"; that would be giving it too much credit. It's just not a song I ever seek out. It's not in my top ten (or twenty, or fifty) favorite Springsteen songs. Those who were with me in Vancouver in 2003 will probably remember my self-righteous indignation (and the vitriolic flow of obscenities) upon hearing a rumor that the evening's performance of "My Hometown" had been an audible[1] and had replaced, of all things, "Incident on 57th Street" on the setlist.[2]

---

1. An audible is a change made to the setlist during a show. "Calling an audible" typically involves Springsteen madly stalking the stage during the closing moments of the previous song and shouting out the title of the song to come. It often results in mass confusion, swift instrument changes and substitutions, and a big goofy grin on Springsteen's face as the band hits the new song right on the button: no hesitation, no prevarication. I suspect that it's not so much Springsteen being caught up by whimsy or reading the mood of the crowd: I think he calls audibles to fuck with the band. Except when he's substituting "My Hometown" for "Incident" in Vancouver: then, I'm pretty sure he's doing it to fuck with me.
2. Ah, "Incident on 57th Street." Or just "Incident," as the fans call it. This is one of my favorite Springsteen songs: top ten for sure, possibly top five. It's a grandiose, intricate,

The music is clunky and monotonous in "My Hometown," and the live versions, they do tend to go on. And on. You can't argue with the sentiment, however, simultaneously plainspoken and borderline overblown though it may be. And therein lies the rub: "My Hometown" speaks to me.

There's a perfect, and beautiful, movement to the song. It begins with the personal—a young boy, the narrator, running out to buy a newspaper for his father—then radiates outward, first to the level of family (with the boy being driven around on his father's lap), then to their community, and then to larger social concerns (the racial tensions of the 1960s, the economic decline of the 1980s) before contracting back to the familial and the personal to finish. This not only allows a panoramic perspective but builds a narrative that spans decades, showing how these social changes have affected individuals: in contrast to the freedom of a boy in a small town running off to the corner store, the "contemporary" characters feel boxed in and are looking for escape. Which leads to the question: is the song's final assertion, "son take a good look around, This is your hometown," with the next-generation repeat of a son driving around on his father's lap, a farewell or a gesture of resignation?

"My Hometown" is a perfect example of what I find most significant about Springsteen's work: his ability to use the specific and the personal (whether true or fictionalized) to create a sense of the universal. In its specific details—newspapers that only cost a dime, a confrontation at a traffic light, the closing of a textile mill—the song resonates for anyone who has grown up in a small town and felt it dying around them.

It certainly resonates for me.

---

operatic epic from Springsteen's second album, and I cannot get enough of it. It is also the one song I've been chasing over more than two decades of concert-going. I've never seen it live, though I've come close a couple of times. The substitution in Vancouver stings to this day, especially since they got it three nights later in Edmonton. Bastards.

A FEW MILES from where the only stoplight in town marks the center of Agassiz proper, out past where the streetlights give way to the darkness, there's a stretch of highway. It's almost the last gasp of the Lougheed, which starts in Vancouver as a major urban thoroughfare, before running into the depths of British Columbia's Fraser Valley, skirting the north side of the river through Port Moody, Coquitlam, and Mission before just bypassing Agassiz and ending up in Hope.

The stretch of highway I'm talking about is little more than a country road: two lanes, pretty quiet most of the time, though on holiday weekends the campers and motorcycles on their way to Harrison Lake can ride bumper to bumper. It's dead straight, that stretch of road, less than a mile long, lined with farms and houses and the skeleton of the old Kent Hotel. It's anchored at one end by the house my mother grew up in, where my grandmother still lives, and on the other by the house my brothers and I were raised in, the house that my father built, now the house my mother lives in with my stepfather, Tom.

When I think of my world as a child, I think of my bedroom, where I hid myself away with my books and my pencils. I think of the hayloft in my grandmother's barn, kittens from the barn cats hiding in the eaves behind the bales, mewing and just out of reach. I think of the forest behind our house, carved with well-beaten trails and bike paths, and of the woods behind my grandmother's place, which were endless, magical, and only slightly terrifying. I think of the tiny elementary school I went to for first and second grades, building forts at lunchtime, kissing Karen in the schoolyard in the spring, and I think of my high school, and the number of times I wanted to burn it to the ground.

Mostly, though, I think of that road.

Our house was on the south side of the road, down a short driveway that looped around a chestnut tree. My father—who was a carpenter—built it from the shell of the old bungalow he and my mother had bought a couple of years after they got married. Some of my earliest memories—little more than fragments, really—are about the gradual emergence of the new house: the way the crumbling patio off the kitchen got covered over by the floorboards of the new family room; an afternoon with my father and his friends and my mother's brothers raising the walls and roof over the second floor; the agonizing process of my father hand-cutting hundreds of angled slats to pattern the walls and floors, the heartbreak, the anger, the beauty. I get my temper from my father. And my propensity for obscenities. The smell of fresh-cut lumber is magical for me; I can't go into a hardware store without feeling like a child again.

My father kept up his industrial first aid certification to give him an edge in the rough job market of the seventies. He worked on a lot of big projects, including one of the prisons they built outside of town, and he was away a lot, weeks at work camps punctuated by weekend visits home.

My mother stayed home with us boys—my two younger brothers, Dave and Jon, and me—until Jon was two, and then she got a job in the accounting office at the Harrison Hotel. Money was tight since my dad was often out of work.

Once the three of us were in school, we would catch the bus to school every morning down at the corner. Mornings were ritualized, in the way that a tight schedule demands: breakfast—the birthday party call-in show on CHWK radio out of Chilliwack—washing up—school bags packed—coats on—out the door by 7:55. We would wait for the bus with the Doran kids from down the road, the Bazan boys, whose parents ran the Kent Hotel, and a few others.

When we got home in the afternoon, it was just the three of us. There was a window at the front of the house, hidden by a shrub, and every day after school we would sneak into the flower bed, slide the window open, and pull ourselves in, closing the window behind us. We were supposed to drop our stuff off, then walk down the road to my grandmother's house, where we would stay until Mom picked us up after work. Some days, though, Dave, Jon, and I would call Mom with a reason to avoid making that trek: maybe it was raining, or one of us wasn't feeling well. Sometimes our excuse actually worked, and we'd stay at the house by ourselves, have a snack, maybe turn on the TV, and occupy ourselves until Mom got home. I usually read. Or wrote.

Most days, though, we would head down the highway at about 3:30. My grandmother would call to check in if we were too late.

Every step of that walk is ingrained in my brain, every foot of that half-mile imbued with memory. We would walk it in all seasons, in all weather. We explored the ditch—looking for frogs and otters when it was full of water, collecting bottles and cans when it was dry, picking blackberries in the summer, pushing each other into the snowy depths in winter. We used the ditch to avoid the big yellow dog that lived—unchained—at the halfway point, sneaking along in silence like a commando unit, breaking into a dead run if we heard the ominous barking.

I hated that dog.

You see, I was born with a clubfoot, which meant, in addition to a number of surgeries and corrective procedures, that I was basically hobbled during my childhood. Oh, I could get around, but to say that I wasn't athletic would be a grave understatement. It also contributed to the fact that I didn't learn to ride a bike until very late, relatively speaking.

Mom and Dad decided when I was nine or ten that it was high time I learned. We dedicated a weekend to the task. And after hours—days—of anguish, I had done it: I was in command of a vehicle, one complete with a banana seat and high handle bars. To mark the occasion, we decided to ride down to Gram's place to show off.

It wasn't a big deal, in theory. The shoulders of the road were wide, Mom was riding behind me with Jon in the carrier seat, and it was a quiet time of day: everything should have been fine. And it was, until we hit the halfway point.

They say dogs can smell fear. That yellow dog must have had a hell of a nose on it, because it tore out of its yard like its tail was on fire, barking furiously as it raced across two lanes of country highway. All I saw was a streak of yellow fur and teeth, with the sound of that barking, and then I felt a crunching as those jaws closed around my left arm. I was already precarious on my banana seat, shakily navigating the asphalt, and when that dog hit me, I went ass over teakettle into the ditch. I lost the bike, and I think the dog got tangled in it and was torn off me. The rest is just a blur.[3]

I hated that dog.

I think I danced when I heard the news that it had been killed on the highway, years later. I hoped he was chasing a kid on a bike when it happened.

But I digress.

The end of the road, for us, was my grandmother's place. It was our second home.

My grandmother was, and is, a pillar of the community. Active in the United Church, she seemed to be friends with everyone in town. There were always cars in her driveway, tea in the pot, and a game on the go on the kitchen table (usually Scrabble or cribbage). Even now when I go back to Agassiz, I'm "Phyllis Eddy's grandson." It was a heavy weight to grow up under: I couldn't get away with anything. Word of even the most innocent of childish troublemaking would work its way to my grandmother with an efficiency that would put Twitter to shame, and ultimately come back to my mother. And, inevitably, me.

Case in point. I spent an afternoon hanging out with Marshall, a kid who lived nearby and was a couple of years older. We rambled through the neighborhood, exploring the ditches and the woods, poking around in forbidden yards. As part of our travels, there was a span of time, maybe two minutes in length—maybe—during which we threw sticks at some crows behind the old Kent Hotel.

---

3. A blur for me, but not for my mother. She recalls coming to a skidding halt, and jumping off her bike and letting it drop at the side of the road to chase the dog away from me. This would have been good for me, but not so good for Jon, still buckled into his seat as the bike hit the pavement.

Sure enough, I arrived at home to my mother asking, "Were you throwing sticks at crows with Marshall?" I was dumbfounded: it had been two minutes, and those crows had been as safe, as my grandmother herself would say, as in the left hand of God. Throwing has never been in my skill set.

Of course, I tried to lie my way out of it. And of course it didn't work.

It was a great time to grow up, and a great place. My brothers and I pretty much had free rein: we rode our bikes everywhere, disappeared into the woods for hours, built forts in the hayloft and the disused, crumbling chicken house. Those times came to an end, though.

At first, the changes happened close to home.

My grandfather died when I was seven. I don't remember him very well, but two memories are crystal clear.

The first is the afternoon that I went with him into Chilliwack[4] to pick up the suits my brother Dave and I were to wear to my aunt's wedding. We had roles in the wedding party that called for matching powder-blue children's tuxedoes, made from a rare polyester found only in the late 1970s. I remember riding with my grandfather in his blue Toyota pickup, the way it shook and shivered as we went over the bridge, as we drove the twenty minutes there and back. I remember talking to him (or, knowing me, talking *at* him) for the length of the drive, and I remember ice cream, probably a Canadian Mint bar (of the ample old-school variety, before they shrank to virtual nothingness, as such things tend to do).

The second memory is of being awakened late one night. My bedroom was at the back of the house, upstairs, alongside the driveway. I heard the sound of the screen door closing, and voices below my window, too quiet for me to make out the words. Voices that I recognized but in my sleep-addled state couldn't place. The screen

---

4. Chilliwack, you have to understand, was the big city if you were from Agassiz: there were a couple of malls, the big grocery stores, and—yes!—a movie theatre.

door opening, then closing again. Engines starting and cars leaving the driveway, cars driving in.

I had to pee, but there was something about the sound of those voices that kept me in bed until I couldn't bear it any more. I snuck out of bed and down the stairs. The lights were on in the kitchen, watery and orange-gold. I hesitated at the foot of the stairs hearing those voices. There had never been a night like this before, and I knew somehow that as soon as I went around the corner, nothing would ever be the same.

It wasn't. My uncle Dan was there, sitting at the table across from my mother, holding her hand as she sobbed. I froze in the doorway, not sure what to do. When my mother finally noticed me, she opened up her arms and tried to smile, explaining that Grandpa had died. I let her hug me, feeling the cold wet of her tears on my neck.

It was the first time I had seen her cry.

It wouldn't be the last.

A few years later, my parents told my brothers and me, over a spaghetti dinner, that they were separating.

From then on, nothing was safe. Nothing was certain. Danger lurked around every corner.

I'd first felt that kind of deep fear in the pit of my belly after the first breakout from the new prisons. There was a warning on the radio, and my mother walked us to the bus stop. Roadblocks stopped traffic, and gun-carrying Mounties searched our school bus first thing.

And then it got worse. In the spring and summer of 1981, the bodies of murdered children and teenagers began to be discovered around the Lower Mainland, several in the area around Harrison Lake, mere minutes up the road. As more and more youths disappeared, my childhood freedom came to an abrupt end: the Clifford Robert Olson killing spree and its aftermath changed life not just in Agassiz but around the province.[5] The woods were no longer a safe haven; they became places of menace, of dangers unseen.[6]

I remember camping that summer, sleeping in the "kids' tent" with Dave and Jon, alongside the daughter of one of my mother's oldest friends and her younger siblings. She was the first girl I can remember having a crush on.[7] After it got dark, with the low voices of our parents almost drowned out by the crackling of the fire, the girl and I whispered about how scared we were. But we shared a great sense of responsibility: we were the oldest in our families. We had a built-in imperative to rise above it. To grow up.

Our childhoods were over.

And in the dark I kissed her, and she kissed me back.

... son take a good look around
This is your hometown

---

5. Olson was arrested in the summer of 1981 and confessed to the murder of eleven children and youths. He was sentenced to eleven concurrent life sentences, and, designated as a dangerous offender, will likely never be released.

6. And it wasn't just the woods, it was the high school as well. Legend had it that Olson had actually been in the school, looking for a telephone, while one of his victims sat outside the library, unaware of her fate. Witnesses claimed she looked like she had been drugged. Whether or not this was true, it was enough to color our lives. I still get a creepy feeling when I look at my graduation group photos, taken at the table where the girl allegedly sat during her last hours.

7. Desperately trying to impress her, I almost drowned (not once, but twice) over the years that followed. She's the reason I became a lifeguard.

It's Hard to be a
Saint in the City

Album: *Greetings from Asbury Park, N.J.*
Released: January 5, 1973
Recorded: July–September 1972
Version discussed: Recorded July 7, 1978, at the Roxy Theatre
Album/released: *Live 1975–85*, November 10, 1986

"IT'S HARD TO be a Saint in the City" is perhaps one of the most significant songs in the Springsteen canon. It sets the tone for his early work, casting a stone of bravado and strut that sends ripples out to "Rosalita" and "Jungleland." It establishes the dynamic of one of his most compelling images (for me, at least): that of our public and private faces.[1] And it gave him a career.

On May 3, 1972, Springsteen walked into CBS Studios in New York to play the most important set of his life, twelve songs to an audience, primarily, of one man: John Hammond, Columbia Records A&R man[2] and talent scout extraordinaire, who was the man credited with "discovering," among others, Billie Holiday,

---

1. In *Songs*, the 1998 book that collects Springsteen's lyrics with commentary from the songwriter, he describes it as one of several songs from his first album that serve as "twisted autobiographies."
2. In music industry parlance, A&R refers to "Artists & Repertoire," the person or division in a record company charged with finding new talent and fostering that talent through the early stages of their career. An A&R person is generally expected to stay abreast of trends and current tastes, with an eye to finding, always, the next big thing. John Hammond was one of the best.

Aretha Franklin, Leonard Cohen, and Bob Dylan.[3] Hammond was impressed, and after seeing how Springsteen interacted with an audience at an open mike that night at the Gaslight—a renowned Manhattan folk club—offered him a contract. He's been on the Columbia roster ever since.

Hammond and label president Clive Davis seem to have thought they were signing the latest in a long line of sensitive singer-songwriters, and their promotion of Springsteen's first record, *Greetings from Asbury Park, N.J.*, was laced with talk of him being a "new Dylan." One of many, many new Dylans at that time.[4]

But Springsteen had The E Street Band as the ace up his sleeve.

The band's presence on the record is noticeable but restrained, nowhere more so than on "Saint." It's definitely a rock song, complete with a great Clemons sax line, but there's something oddly tasteful about it. The E Street Band sounds tight, but almost polite.[5] There's nothing in that song, or on the album,[6] to hint at just how intense and overwhelming the band could be live. They were burning it up on stage (case in point, their 1975 appearance at the Hammersmith Odeon in London, now officially available on DVD[7]), but little more than background on the record. The band's power later comes through in spades on the version of "Saint" from the *Live 1975–85* box set, recorded at the Roxy in L.A. in July 1978 and released with a stunning amount of publicity just in time for Christmas 1986.[8]

---

3. Dylan was actually referred to as "Hammond's folly" in the Columbia corridors, until he became, well, Bob fucking Dylan.

4. Springsteen, as one might expect, chafed at the comparison.

5. Or possibly constrained by the limitations of 914 Sound Studios.

6. Or on any Springsteen album, really. It's been said of the Grateful Dead that they were really two bands, and if you wanted to get it you had to see them live. The dichotomy isn't quite as extreme with Springsteen and the E Street Band; there are songs in the studio catalogue that give a sense of the band's power in a live setting, but nothing really captures it. You really *do* have to see them live to get it.

7. Note the "officially" here. There are some great, great bootleg recordings of shows and radio sessions pre-Hammersmith, if you know where to look, including one of the all-time best Springsteen shows, from the rightly celebrated Bottom Line gigs of August 1975.

It's hard to avoid getting swept up by Springsteen himself, but listen to how unhinged the band is, racing through what was originally a relatively sedate, relatively acoustic song.[9] This is the sound of The E Street Band vintage 1978, playing as if their lives depended on it. As tight as James Brown's Fabulous Flames, as raw and urgent as The Clash, this is the band at its absolute peak.[10]

For me though, it's mostly about the words. Check out those lyrics. You can almost picture the narrator, can't you?[11] He's suave, he's cool, he's hard and confident; he's got the whole city at his feet. Cock of the walk, a prince among men. As Springsteen has said of Clarence Clemons many times over the years, "You want to be him, but you can't." You've probably never met someone quite as cool as the narrator of "It's Hard to be a Saint in the City."

You've certainly never heard anyone extolling his own cool to quite this extreme, at any rate.

And really, that's the key. If you're truly cool, you don't talk about it—you let other people do that. That's one of the hallmarks of being cool, isn't it? This guy can't shut up about it.

And then Springsteen hits you with the punchline: he's not all he claims. He's "just a boy out on the street."

The song, save for that one line, documents the construction of a mask, a façade. It's the first of Springsteen's façade songs, and

8. The *Live* box set is a fantastic artifact, and you can't possibly quibble with what it contains: forty tracks of live Springsteen, at a time when only a handful of live recordings had been officially released. However. It's also one of those releases that has fans wondering, to this day, "What the fuck were they thinking?" For starters? They cut the "Sad Eyes/Drive All Night" passage from the recording of "Backstreets." One of the most haunting, intense moments in Springsteen history, and they cut it?

9. Completely acoustic, if you go back to the original Hammond demos.

10. So strongly do I feel about the 1978 tour that I considered at one point attempting to collect bootlegs of every show. Why, you might ask? Tell you what: listen to *Pièce de Résistance*, *Live at the Roxy*, *Summertime Blues*, and *Live in the Promised Land* and see if you still need to inquire. I think you'll see the wisdom of the plan.

11. If you're like me, you *can* picture the narrator. "Saint" was used to great effect in John Sayles's film *Baby, It's You*, as background for a breathless first glimpse of the tough male lead, the Sheik, played with slicked-back, leathered glory by Vincent Spano. Try as I might, I can't shake that image. It doesn't, however, detract from what I'm about to say.

once you're aware of the theme, and of Springsteen's personal experience with hiding in plain sight as a child and teenager, you have to wonder: if he's trying that hard to create an alternate persona, what's that boy trying to hide? Who is he trying to fool?

I WAS NEVER a popular kid. Not from day one.

I was sheltered from it for a while: for grades one and two I went to McCaffrey school, a two-room schoolhouse with maybe fifty students. We were a relatively close-knit group, and everyone seemed to get along pretty well. That was where I learned to read, and where I started to write, making up stories in my head to explain the terrible pictures I attempted to draw.

The transition to third grade was jarring: we moved en masse to Kent Elementary, which went up to grade six. Damn, those were some big kids. In a big school. And me...with, really, nothing to offer.

It's easy, growing up in a small town, to develop an inferiority complex if you can't play sports and you aren't interested in watching them.[12] You're essentially cut off from the mainstream culture. More so if you're a bookworm, the sort of kid who sits on the bus jotting notes into notebooks and writing stories at lunchtime. Even more so if you're a shy kid in purple corduroy pants.[13]

I was, as they say, out of my element.

Which would have been bad enough. I could have been one of those kids nobody notices, the ones who fade into the wallpaper, people you don't remember until they show up at your high school reunion, beautiful and tanned and rich. I could have been one of those kids.

But no, that would have been too easy.

---

12. To paraphrase a great Tragically Hip song, no, I didn't give a fuck about hockey. And in Agassiz, they'd never heard anyone say that before.

13. I'm not going to tell the story of the purple cords. It's an involved, painful tale of hand-me-downs and church rummage sales, set to that infernal swish-swish-swish noise. I haven't worn cords of any color since third grade, the scars run so deep. But catch me on a night when I've had too much to drink and maybe I'll tell you the story. Because there's nothing I like more when I'm drinking than making people cry.

I didn't want to be wallpaper. If I couldn't fit in, I was going to stand out.[14] So I embraced what I had.

I had always been a smart kid, but I started to let my classmates know it. I always had an answer, and a cutting remark, and an attitude. I became arrogant, condescending, and self-righteous. In order to avoid anonymity, I made myself insufferable.[15] I can admit that now.

But you know what? Nobody deserves the treatment I got. No one.

I was beaten up in the schoolyard. I was harassed on the bus and walking down the halls. I was jumped both when I was dreading it and when I least expected it.

And it wasn't just the kids. There were teachers who were almost as bad. Partway through grade four, I fell while running backward in gym class, and something snapped in my arm. The teacher refused to consider that anything was wrong, and scorned me for crying. I showed up the next day in a cast: I had broken my wrist.

I did make it worse for myself, in some ways. I never hesitated, for example, to lie. And lie boldly. In third grade, shortly before St. Patrick's Day, I claimed that I had kissed the Blarney Stone, having grown up in Ireland as I had. It took my teacher, Miss Guthrie, about fifteen minutes to confirm that I was full of crap, which knowledge she proceeded to eviscerate me with in front of my class, without mercy. I can't really blame her[16]—she was a teacher, and teaching moral behavior was probably part of her code—but it was the worst thing that could have happened from a Rob-getting-his-ass-kicked point of view.

That was the low point, until the beginning of grade four.

Grade four... I shiver just thinking about it.

Mid-August, two weeks before school went back, my mother

---

14. Understand, this wasn't a rational process. Had I given it even a moment's thought, I would have faded into the wallpaper and saved myself five or six years of torment.
15. Thankfully, I grew out of that. No, really. All right, shut up.
16. And clearly I've forgiven her: she's one of three teachers thanked in the acknowledgements in my novel *Before I Wake*.

and I took a trip to Chilliwack. In the course of a single afternoon, I visited the dentist and the optometrist. I got glasses and braces the same day.

I'll let that sink in before adding that was the summer I started to grow hair in fun places, and discovered just how fun those places could be.

Cut ahead to the first day of school. New glasses, new braces, in the first bloom of puberty? I was like chum in a tank too full of sharks. I got ripped apart.

And that lasted for four years.

It's easy to be glib about it now. Time blunts the pain and the reality. You can explain it away and make excuses. You can create punchlines. But it wasn't easy. In fact, I barely survived.

At the end of grade six, my classmates and I moved to the high school. Grades seven through twelve. Damn, those were some big kids. In a big school. And me... with, really, nothing to offer.

Everything that had been wrong in elementary school was worse. And there were new horrors: lockers to be slammed against or into; bigger bullies, and more of them; isolated corners of a (relatively) huge building to be savaged in.

And gym class.

Even worse, though, were the change rooms. Mandatory showers after gym class. When I imagine Hell, it looks an awful lot like the boys' change room at Agassiz Secondary.[17]

Through it all, I put up a front. I created someone else, so that no one would see how I was hurting. How this was killing me.

Thirteen is too old to be crying yourself to sleep every night.

And it's too young to be standing in the bathroom thinking that maybe the razor blade wouldn't hurt that much as you ran it up the inside of your wrist (not across... you want to do it right).

---

17. I admit I brought some of this torment on myself. It is not, for example, a good idea to point out that the penis of the fourteen-year-old bully about to kick the crap out of you in the change room shower is curiously small and hairless for someone of his size and age. Let's call that a lesson I learned the hard way.

No one knew how I hurt, and how much I wanted to die. And no one knew how much I wanted to kill. The stories I wrote back then would have me arrested today. But I confined my bully-cide and school burnings to the page.

And no one ever knew.

I created a mask, one that looked a lot like me. This persona, this arrogant, self-righteous, infuriating Rob? That was the part of me people hit.

Nobody could touch the real me.

And you know what saved my life?

Since you've been reading this far, it shouldn't come as a surprise.

Rock and roll.

Heavy metal, to be specific. Black Sabbath, Iron Maiden. I never really got into Judas Priest, but I wore the t-shirts.

Really, it was all about the t-shirts.

There is nothing like heavy metal for the consummate outsider. It's the music of misfits, of clumsy kids and the socially disjointed. There's a heroism to it, honor among the down and out.

In 1983, in Agassiz, when you wore a Black Sabbath *Mob Rules* t-shirt, the one splattered with blood and decorated with post-massacre body parts, you were self-identifying as an outsider. When you put on an Iron Maiden *Piece of Mind* shirt, the one with the pie slice cut out of the brain, you were pledging allegiance to the world of not-fitting-in. You had officially hit the point where you didn't give a fuck, and you didn't care who knew it.

So I started growing my hair, and I wore the t-shirts, and something stunning happened. The beatings stopped. The persecution stopped. The pain stopped.

Within a few weeks, a lot of the older kids were calling me Ozzy.[18] I was greeted as people passed. I was high-fived. And some

---

18. I don't need to explain that the nickname came from Ozzy Osbourne, former lead singer of Black Sabbath, then infamous for the rumor that he bit the head off a live dove, do I?

of those older kids stood up for me now when the bullies started in on me.

The trouble was, that don't-give-a-shit heavy metal kid wasn't me. The real me was still locked somewhere inside.

When I think about those days, I remember the ass-kickings and the torment. I remember the taunting, the incessant laughter.[19] And I remember feeling so, so alone.

But I did have friends. One friend in particular.

Peter.[20]

Peter moved to Agassiz from Sardis, a suburb of Chilliwack, the summer before grade four. I met him on the first day of school. He was a tall, gangly kid, glasses and a funny haircut, from a strict German family. He wore his shirts buttoned to the very top, and we sat together near the back of Mr. Fraser's class.

We hit it off immediately, two geeks at the back, and our friendship has never flagged, despite the thousands of miles between us. He's still tall, and he's still got glasses, but he's grown into that gangliness.

Peter suffered a lot of the same persecution I did,[21] but he developed coping strategies that kept him largely from the brunt of it, an approach that largely boiled down to "not being there." He lived in town, so he'd arrive in the morning just before the bell, he went home for lunch every day, and he disappeared right after school.

Smart lad, that Peter.

The dynamic we had then is pretty much what we continue to have. He's the wise one, and I'm the smart-ass; he hangs back and I plunge in, persona-first. I'm the one who gets into trouble, and he's... well, he's right there with me. Your friends, your true friends, are the ones you wake up in jail with.[22]

---

19. To this day, the sound of teenage girls laughing on a bus will cause an adrenaline spike and a fight-or-flight reaction. Hence the music during my commute.
20. I told you you'd meet Peter. Wasn't that a good entrance?
21. It just occurred to me: he might actually have suffered from some of that persecution *because* of me. I suppose I owe him an apology. And a drink.
22. Metaphorically speaking. Really.

Those days were ahead of us, though. Grades four through eight?
Well, we survived. That's about as much as can be said.

The devil appeared like Jesus through the steam in the street
Showin' me a hand I knew even the cops couldn't beat
I felt his hot breath on my neck as I dove into the heat
It's so hard to be a saint when you're just a boy out on the street

Badlands

Album: *Darkness on the Edge of Town*
Released: June 2, 1978
Recorded: October 12, 1977–March 19, 1978

SPRINGSTEEN FANS ARE a weird lot.[1] It's not just the devotion, the inexorable pull that draws us away from home, that has us happily spending twelve hours in a general admission line and referring to each other by nicknames drawn from one Springsteen song or another.[2]

No, those things are relatively normal, as far as devoted fans go.[3] What strikes me as odd about Springsteen fans is our masochism. It's the way we grow, largely by process of overexposure—which we ourselves are responsible for—to revile the songs we love most. Familiarity, for us, breeds contempt. I'm not talking about songs from *Born in the U.S.A.*; no self-respecting Tramp[4] is likely to claim any of those as his favorite, save for possibly the title track.

No, I'm talking about songs that genuinely move our souls, that are key, in many ways, to our fandom, and that we eventually come to loathe.

---

1. As she reads that sentence, I'm sure Cori is nodding and muttering something about "an understatement."
2. I made that last one up. I've never met any Springsteen fan who has a nickname based on a song. Ask my friend G-man; he'll back up his old pal Wild Billy.
3. And we've got nothing on Trekkies. Man, those people are nuts.
4. Oh, right. We have a label: Tramps. It's not as catchy as Deadheads or Phishheads (or Trekkies), but hey, it's from one of the great lines in "Born to Run," and it's hard to argue with that.

Take "Badlands" as an example.

The opening track on *Darkness on the Edge of Town*, "Badlands" was most people's first glimpse of the new Bruce Springsteen. He was still recovering from his bitter legal battle with his former manager, Mike Appel, which had kept him from releasing new music for three years, and *Darkness* revealed a songwriter tortured and ground down.

Darkness is a mature record, by design. Gone are the anthems of escape, like "Thunder Road" and "Born to Run." Rather than jumping in a car and running, the characters in *Darkness* are trapped, consigned to late-night road races and early mornings waking to the factory's whistle. Exploring loss of faith, loss of love, succor in sex, and weekend thrill-taking, the album is a masterpiece of ennui verging on despair. Sure, there's defiance there, but it's a bitter and impotent railing against reality.

Springsteen wasn't even thirty years old when *Darkness* was released, and it sounded as if the world had already broken him.

This was, in fact, a deliberate choice on Springsteen's part. In the book *Songs*, he writes, "After *Born to Run* I wanted to write about life in the close confines of the small towns I grew up in... I intentionally steered away from any hint of escapism and set my characters down in the middle of a community under siege."[5]

As a result of that deliberateness (some would say ruthlessness), the songs on *Darkness*—each of them a masterpiece—have some of the best staying power in Springsteen's canon. A typical Springsteen concert, even more than thirty years later, will feature four

---

5. In November, 2010, Springsteen released *The Promise: The Darkness on the Edge of Town Story*, a three CD/three DVD set that explores the genesis of the album, and, most strikingly, how deliberately Springsteen had created paths not taken. In the break between *Born to Run* and *Darkness*, Springsteen wrote more than seventy songs; ten were selected for the album. With the outtakes on *Tracks* and the two CDs worth in the box set, more than forty of those songs have been made available, and it's easy to see the method to his madness: even great songs like "Because the Night" and "The Promise" were dropped because they didn't fit his vision of the record. Given the results, it's hard to quibble.

or five tracks from the album. The title track, "The Promised Land," "Candy's Room," "Prove It All Night," and "Racing in the Street" are all in regular rotation even now.[6]

It's a curious alchemy, what these songs do to a sold-out arena of fans. Take the title track. "Darkness on the Edge of Town" is utterly despairing, a chronicle of a man who's lost his money and his wife and no longer cares. He lives for weekend nights when he can race in the darkness and lay what little he has on the line. In concert, though, the song becomes a communal moment, a shared cry of frustration. Let's face it: there are a lot of lives that feel like dead ends, and many people live for the moments that take them out of that life-as-mere-survival mindset. A Springsteen concert, say. "Darkness" is a raised voice of understanding, twenty thousand strong, every night. That shared experience transmutes despair to a true measure of defiance.

The same is true of "Badlands." In concert, especially since the 1999–2000 reunion tour, it's become a regular setpiece. The house lights are turned up partway, and the song transforms into a sing-along, often with several minutes of milked audience response. And it works. Of course it works. On the *Live in Barcelona* DVD you can see the intensity of the crowd reaction, the surging, roiling sea of hands, hear the voices raised in song almost overpowering the band. It's remarkable, and moving.

And Tramps, generally speaking? We hate it.

It's not the disappointment we share in a 2003 version of "Prove It All Night" that will never hold a candle to the epic versions of the

---

6. One of the best parts about the *Darkness* box set? In late 2009 Springsteen and a stripped-down version of The E Street Band—essentially the same band who recorded the album, with Charlie Giordano subbing on organ for the late Danny Federici—set up on stage at the Paramount Theatre in Asbury Park and ran through the album, from "Badlands" to the title track, performing to an empty theatre. It's stunning just how deeply these songs are still felt, how much passion Springsteen brings to tracks like "Badlands." He could be forgiven, having performed them hundreds of times, if he was bored with them. Yet there's no boredom here, just the sheer, undiluted power of the music.

1978 tour, no matter how strong it is. Nor is it the disdain we have for later versions of "Thunder Road," tainted by what some fans call "the twang."

No, this is a case of hating what you love, plain and simple. Because every one of those people who bitches on message boards about what a warhorse "Badlands" has become, how bloated and overblown, how much it panders to the audience, I guarantee you: every one of those people, when the song rolls around in concert, will have their hands in the air and tears in their eyes. They'll strain their vocal cords, and experience, for a moment, transcendence.

And then they'll log on again and complain about how it slowed down the show, and ask things like "Why isn't he playing 'Be True' or 'None But the Brave' in that slot?"

It's the curse of being a Tramp.

I know it well.

IF YOU WERE a kid growing up in the country (and make no mistake, Agassiz was and is country, through and through[7]), a summer job generally meant misery. Outdoor misery, regardless of the weather. "Workin' in the fields, till you get your back burned," as Springsteen sings in "Badlands."

Options for summer work tended to come down to word of mouth: so-and-so knew somebody who was looking for a few young guys to spend a couple of days bringing the hay in. So-and-so was looking for someone to dig something out or cut something down or pick something or plant something or bury something. Work-wise, you were largely limited to a choice between brutal and humiliating. I had the bad fortune, for a few years, of working summer jobs that bridged the gap.

I'd be hard-pressed to say which is worse, picking strawberries or picking corn. If you're picking strawberries, you're either hunched

---

7. You know what the dividing line is between "country town" and "town," let alone "city"? A movie theatre.

over, killing your back, or kneeling in the dew-soaked mud. Picking corn, you get to stand up, but your shoulders are rubbed bloody with the burlap sack you're picking into, and you spend hours crashing between rows of plants wet with dew, so you end up soaked to the skin, sweating and chilled before the August sun is even up. Picking corn, you rip your hands apart on the razor edges of the leaves. Picking strawberries, you get covered in strawberry juice, which only *sounds* fun; it takes you an hour in the shower at night to get the sugary mud off. Picking corn, you get yelled at for selecting unripe cobs; with strawberries, it's the "goddamn monkey faces" your boss picks out of your basket and throws over his shoulder, shorting your weight. They're both dawn-hour studies in endurance.

If I had to choose, I suppose I'd say picking strawberries is a little less onerous than picking corn, for a couple of reasons. First, it's never a bad thing to sneak a glowing, ripe strawberry right off the vine. You can't say that about an ear of corn, no matter how sweet. Second, picking corn was a solo endeavor; picking strawberries, I got to work with Greg.

Unlike Peter, whom I can recall meeting, Greg Lawley was from town, and I'd known him all my life. He was hard to miss: even as a kid he was almost terrifyingly tall, and to this day he stands, literally, a foot higher than I do. With height like that, Greg was a natural for basketball, and from an early age he was inseparable from his ball. Many summer nights we'd spend hours on the outdoor court at the high school. We never played HORSE or anything like that—he'd position and take a shot, I'd grab the ball and send it back his way. Badly. Repeatedly.

I don't remember how Greg and I became friends, exactly, but it was sometime in grade eight or nine. At our high school, the clichéd line between jocks and nerds didn't really exist.[8] Greg was a

---

8. The big social division seemed to be between bullies and the people they picked on; everyone else was pretty harmonious.

basketball player, but there was never any issue with the two of us hanging out, and before long other team members—Kevin, Victor, and John—were part of my social circle, which also included Peter, Jeff, Brendan. And a few girls: Nicole and Jennifer, Deanna, Rose-anne and Karen. And there was Shawna. But more on her later. We would hang out outside the gym in the morning before school, or in the library, or, later, in the stairwell.

Greg and I bonded over two things. The first was, oddly enough, cooking. The second was music.

In a school as small as ours, electives were hard to come by. I ended up in home ec largely by process of elimination; Greg fol-lowed me there for a few years. We made a terrible partnership as far as the class work went (I remember some ghastly dishes, and a general air of disaster surrounding us[9]), but we had some great con-versations while we cooked. We talked mostly[10] about music.

At that time, coming out of my heavy metal t-shirt phase, we talked a lot about bands like Quiet Riot and Twisted Sister.[11] And we talked about Springsteen.

Around then, it was all *Born in the U.S.A.* The album had charged into the public consciousness to the point where there was no avoiding it, but we were proud to be riding the front edge of that wave. Listen to it on the radio? Perish the thought! We had our own cassettes.

And then I had to have surgery.

One of the lingering effects of my clubfoot was that I had uneven bone growth in my legs. To wit, my left leg was shorter than my right. In the first consultation about the issue with my doctor in Vancouver, I was informed that we needed to wait until I had hit bone maturity (i.e., had finished growing), and then we'd take care

---

9. I stuck with home ec for the duration of my high school days; in fact, I was the top student five years running. I've got certificates and everything.

10. "Mostly" is an important word here. It means I don't have to acknowledge the fact that Greg and I knew an uncomfortable amount about each other's masturbation habits and girlie magazine consumption at a tender age.

11. I know, I know, not really heavy metal: we were fourteen! We were the demographic.

of the problem.[12] He sent me for X-rays and booked a follow-up for a month later.

I left his office on Granville and Sixteenth with my mom, heading downtown. She had plans in Vancouver that night, and I was taking the bus back to Agassiz. En route to the bus station we stopped at A&B Sound. I bought a few tapes, including *The Wild, the Innocent & the E Street Shuffle*.

It was the second Springsteen album I owned, and I bought it because it had "Rosalita" on it, but the rest of the tape blew my mind. The wild cacophony that kicked off "The E Street Shuffle" was like a hurdy-gurdy unhinged, so far removed from the slick blue-collar rock of *Born in the U.S.A.* it was like a different band altogether.

Greg and I spent hours playing pool on the table in my living room[13] and cranking the tape as loud as it would go. We pieced together the lyrics and sang along. We studied it with the dedication of Talmudic scholars.[14]

A month later, after my follow-up with my doctor, I once again ended up in downtown Vancouver, prowling the record stores. I bought a bunch more tapes at A&B Sound, but the real discovery was a record store well into the shady section of Granville Street. When I walked in, I thought I had gone to heaven: facing the door, there was a rack loaded with bootlegs.[15]

---

12. By "take care of the problem," it turns out my doctor meant "cut an inch of bone out of your right thigh to make it the same length as the left." As someone who was never going to be tall, the loss of that inch wounds me deeply, to this day.

13. The secondhand pool table was a Christmas gift for Dave, Jon, and me, to encourage us to make friends and have them over.

14. There was something utterly messed up about that tape. In order to conserve resources and make for a better playing experience (i.e., no lengthy silence at the end of one side), the geniuses at Columbia had decided to change the running order to balance the two sides of the cassette. As a result, I didn't actually hear *Wild and Innocent* the way it was intended—with that gorgeous second-side suite of "Incident on 57th Street," "Rosalita," and "New York City Serenade" until at least a decade later, when I bought a copy on CD. Of all the second sides in rock history, that one might just be the finest.

15. Ah, bootlegs. Live concert recordings or purloined studio tracks, pressed on crappy vinyl in dubious European locales.

I knew all about bootlegs. Greg and I had been trading books about Springsteen back and forth for months, and it was impossible to avoid awareness of the fact that Springsteen was—and remains—one of the most bootlegged artists of all time. Much of his popularity, and the legends about his live shows, stem from recordings of radio broadcasts (the August 15, 1975, show at the Bottom Line in New York and the December 15, 1978, show at Winterland in San Francisco, to name the two most significant) that passed from hand to hand and were sold at disreputable record shops, outside concerts, and at flea markets. Before the internet, a lot of being a Springsteen fan involved exchanging tapes by mail, spreading the wealth, building a community.

That day? To actually come across bootlegs, though? It was like being welcomed into the kingdom.

The titles were unfamiliar, but the sleeves hinted at the arcane riches within.

The bootlegs were outrageously expensive, of course, but they beckoned me like a drug. When he saw me looking, picking up the albums one by one like they were fragile, the guy behind the counter let me know that, if I was interested, he might be able to do something for me. Just like any good dealer would. He gestured at a wall of cassettes behind him, all encased in white paper sleeves, with hand-typed titles. He had tapes of all the vinyl bootlegs in the store, and more.

Over the next few months, Greg and I built a wicked bootleg tape collection. We started with the Alpine Valley show from 1984 and part of the Agora, Cleveland, show from 1978. The latter was the one that destroyed us, that turned us from fans into Tramps: the energy level was off the charts, and suddenly everything that we had heard and read, all those legends and rumors, was inarguably true.

When Jack, the hulking Dutchman[16] who was renting my grandmother's west field to grow strawberries, let her know he was

---

16. Cleverly, his nickname was "Dutch."

looking for someone to pick and sell the berries, I was a natural choice. I selected Greg as my wingman and partner in crime.

The strawberry season lasted just a few weeks every year, late June into early July. Greg and I would meet up at dawn and ride our bikes down the highway to my grandmother's field. We'd pick in side-by-side rows, talking music and girls, and talking Bruce.

When the picking was done, we'd man our roadside stand, stretched out in lawn chairs, listening to tapes, reading from Bruce bios or music magazines, nipping up to my grandmother's house for food and drink. It was a relationship forged in work and frustration and music.

And we felt part of a community that expanded far beyond us. One photocopied fanzine, almost a year out of date, featured, among other things, lyrics to songs that had been played late in the *Born in the U.S.A.* tour but hadn't been recorded, songs like "Seeds" and "This Hard Land." Songs of the earth, the misery of work, and the healing balm of companionship. It was all right there, our summer, the backbreaking labor and drudgery, shared by people around the world, having been transformed by a now-less-scrawny singer from New Jersey.

> *Workin' in the fields*
> *till you get your back burned*
> *Workin' 'neath the wheel*
> *till you get your facts learned*
> *Baby I got my facts*
> *learned real good right now*

Born to Run

Album: *Born to Run*
Released: August 25, 1975
Recorded: 1974–75

IT COULD BE ARGUED[1] that Bruce Springsteen's career revolves around two poles. I'm not talking about his music, I'm talking about his decades as a performing artist, and the public awareness of his music. It's an oversimplification, of course, but what Springsteen's career comes down to, for the vast majority of listeners, are two songs and the albums to which they give their names: "Born to Run," and "Born in the U.S.A."

As I've mentioned, *Born in the U.S.A.* and its first single, "Dancing in the Dark," broke upon a largely unsuspecting MTV generation in 1984. The move from arenas to stadiums, international superstardom, the attempted political co-opting of his message: this was Springsteen in the mid-1980s.

A decade earlier, though, there wasn't even a hint of this future. Following the release and disappointing sales of his second album *The Wild, the Innocent & the E Street Shuffle*, Springsteen's career as a major-label artist[2] hung precariously in the balance. His next album was a make-or-break proposition, and the pressure brought out the best and the worst in him.

---

1. Watch me, I'm about to do it.
2. This being the 1970s, before the rise of the indie rock underground, you were either a major-label artist or you were in a bar band, playing on the weekends within an easy drive of your house. There was no in-between.

Springsteen and the touring version of The E Street Band, which then included David Sancious on keyboards, Ernest "Boom" Carter on drums, and Suki Lahav on violin, recorded the lead-off single, a song called "Born to Run," between gigs over a period of almost six months in mid-1974.

Let me repeat that: they recorded the single—one song—over a period of almost six months.

The process, which is documented to thrilling effect in the *Wings for Wheels* documentary included in the *Born to Run: 30th Anniversary* box set, was excruciating. Springsteen adopted a Phil Spector-esque wall of sound approach to the song, layering instrumental track after instrumental track until everyone in the production booth lost track of how many guitars were appearing at any given time.[3] And yes, that is a glockenspiel you hear. Springsteen had a sound in his head—as he so often seems to—and he wasn't relenting until he captured it on tape. It was only after Jon Landau was brought into the fold as a somewhat detached observer and advisor that Springsteen was finally able to let go.

When the song was finished in November 1974, Mike Appel "leaked" an almost finished version to a few influential deejays in loyal Springsteen markets (Boston, Cleveland, Philadelphia, New York). Not only did they take to the anthem, but its popularity brought songs from the first two albums back to the airwaves, and started the ball of hype rolling.

That hype would explode the following summer, when the release of the album was greeted with simultaneous *Time* and *Newsweek* magazine covers, radio broadcasts of live shows, and arduous touring.

Despite a backlash—the inevitable questioning of record company machinations, the skepticism ("Is it really as good as all that?"), and Springsteen's own discomfort with being in the spotlight

---

3. An effect that has been replicated live over the last decade's worth of tours to considerably less positive effect. Seriously—how many guitarists does a band need? Surely the four or five of Springsteen's recent tours are excessive?

anywhere other than on stage[4]—the album clearly did what it was supposed to: it made Bruce Springsteen a star.

But what of the title track itself? You've heard it so many times, but when was the last time you actually listened to it?

Musically, the song is at the same time stunningly beautiful and a bit of an overproduced mess.[5] Dense and heady, layered and propulsive, it is practically the archetypal rock anthem.

"Born to Run" is, self-consciously, a song of defiance and escape. It was released at the pinnacle of Springsteen's early "romantic" period, which was marked by larger-than-life characters (with great nicknames), epic storytelling, and dense soundscapes. The streets of smalltown New Jersey were too small to contain the lives and the dreams of his characters, and they blew out of the place with their car radios blaring.

Live, the song is the moment in every concert where everything comes together. The houselights go up, and the crowd becomes part of the show.[6] It's a ritualized gesture toward community, the breaking down of the wall between performer and audience. When Springsteen calls out "Tramps like us, baby we were born to run," that "we" is all ten, twenty, fifty thousand of us.[7]

---

4. His distaste for the hype was so intense that, upon arriving in London prior to his first English shows—one of which is documented on the *Hammersmith Odeon* DVD— Springsteen grew enraged at the billboards announcing "At last, London is ready for Bruce Springsteen!" and the leaflets on every seat at the concert hall. He famously tore down every poster with his picture on it he encountered. He has, since then, gotten considerably more comfortable with hype.

5. I suppose it depends on how you feel about heavily orchestrated, wall of sound studio products versus live from the floor recordings.

6. If you ever happen to be at a Springsteen show, clinging to the lip of the stage, you should spend at least part of "Born to Run" with your back to the band, facing out into the audience. The crowd seems to become a living, unified organism, and to witness that while being a part of it is an experience almost religious in its intensity.

7. Springsteen has, in recent years, tried to replicate that moment with the mass singalong, houselights on, to "Badlands." It's a similar moment, but nowhere near as powerful: for many fans, "Born to Run" is *the* song, and that moment of a concert is singular and unmatched.

On the *Tunnel of Love* tour in early 1988, Springsteen stripped the song down to its fundamentals. Stepping to the center of a dark stage for his first encore, with a harmonica rack around his neck and cradling an acoustic guitar, Springsteen launched into a monologue about an unnamed song he said had "changed a lot over the years." The song had once seemed to be about escape, but now it seemed to him to be more about searching. Running to, not running away from.

In its acoustic form, "Born to Run" has a mournful quality unimaginable in the full-band version. There is a weariness to the lyrics, a desperation. It's a song haunted by loss and regret, and when the narrator cries out, "I want to know if love is wild, Girl I want to know if love is real," the words are no longer exultant. Rather, they seem like a plea to the universe, a desperate last grasp to find meaning. What lies out there at the end of the road? Where are these people going? What will they find?

The absence of answers hangs in the air.

WHEN YOU become a parent, you immediately start to question your life and your past actions. Would I urge Xander to follow in all of my footsteps? Never. Getting high in a hillside cemetery on a summer night? Not for my boy. Losing the bulk of his first year at university drunk, as a coping mechanism? Please no.

You spend time questioning your own parents and their decisions, too. What, for example, possessed my mother to allow her seventeen-year-old son to buy scalped tickets and accept a ride from a complete stranger to a Springsteen show in a foreign country, hundreds of miles from home?[8]

---

8. I asked my mother this very question a few weeks ago. I assumed she would say something along the lines of, "Well, you were very mature for your age, and I knew if there were any problems you'd be able to think your way out of them and act responsibly." Well, she sort of said that. What she really said was "Actually you've been pretty self-sufficient since birth and you did whine and cajole A LOT!! I just inherently felt that it would be okay and you were capable of looking out for yourself. However, there may have been difficulties that I'm not aware of, and even now, I'm not sure I want to know!" Mom, you might want to skip this chapter.

It was spring 1988. Springsteen was on the *Tunnel of Love* tour,[9] and Peter and I were a month away from graduating from high school. The tour wasn't coming to Vancouver, but it *was* going to hit Tacoma, just south of Seattle. I was hardcore at that point (or at least I thought I was), and there was no way I was going to miss it.

CFOX, one of the Vancouver radio stations, had chartered some buses to take people down to the show, but the tickets were ridiculously expensive, too rich for my blood, by far. So I spent days poring over classified ads in the Vancouver *Province*, looking for scalpers' tickets to the sold-out show, running up a huge long-distance bill and X-ing out ads when I discovered the tickets were already sold. I figured I would get tickets first, then worry about how we were going to get to the Tacoma Dome, almost two hundred miles away.

Both of those questions resolved themselves when I lucked into an informal scalper in Richmond, a Vancouver suburb. Dan[10] worked at a record store, and he had ended up with a couple of extra tickets. He was going to the show himself, and he seemed like a nice enough guy, so I asked (ah, naive bloom of a smalltown boy) if he'd be willing to give us a ride to the show.

He said yes.[11]

I can't remember exactly how I sold the idea to my mother. Peter's response when I asked him recently how he presented the plan to his mom? "I think I lied."

We met Dan at the record store where he worked. Almost immediately, we knew he was the coolest guy we had ever encountered. Dan worked in a record store! Dan had a girlfriend! Dan had his own apartment! Dan had his own car![12]

---

9. The t-shirts were captioned "This is not a dark ride"—the t-shirts lied.
10. I have no idea if "Dan" is his actual name, but I need to use something, right?
11. The fan in me says, of course, "Cool." My parental side, though, keeps repeating something along the lines of "Are you kidding me?"
12. In retrospect, of course, Dan was just a young guy, probably only a couple of years older than we were, working a shitty retail job, with a shitty car that was only barely going to make it to Tacoma, with a girlfriend who was ... well, let's not get ahead of ourselves.

We hung around in the record store, searching in vain for bootlegs while Dan finished out his shift. It was drizzling as we walked across the parking lot to his car, a little Honda that was sporty and sleek and everything that a guy like Dan would have.

We barely even registered the hole in the roof.

In the same way, it would take us a bit to notice that the rest of Dan's life wasn't quite what we'd imagined. His apartment? A crappy one-bedroom, the sort of apartment in which someone can die one day, and it's only a matter of hosing off the vinyl couch and putting a new plastic cover on the mattress before the place is back on the market the next.[13]

Dan's car? Falling apart, with a roaring, whining engine and a funky smell inside that we couldn't quite identify. And yes, that hole in the roof, patched with plastic and duct tape.

His girlfriend?[14]

Dan's girlfriend was waiting at his apartment, and she was upset. The kind of upset that quickly turned into crying. She didn't want to go to the show. Peter and I stood in the hallway while Dan and his girlfriend fought. And fought. And fought. But finally she relented, and we all piled into the car, headed for the border.

In the backseat, I exchanged a look with Peter. A cautious smile. It was happening. Our plan was coming together, and we were on the road. Nothing could stop us now.

"You're gonna need to hold that down," Dan said as we were about to merge onto the freeway.

"What?" asked Peter, who was sitting behind him.

"The plastic," Dan said, without turning around. "It's gonna come loose once we get on the highway. Just roll down the window and hold it down."

Peter, to his credit, didn't balk. Out loud, at least. The look he shot me, though, as he rolled down the window and hooked his arm out into the rain to hold down the patch over the hole in the roof was...

---

13. The apartment was a lot like the one I lived in my first year out of student housing in Victoria.

14. Let's call her, in the absence of any memory of her real name, Dana.

Well, it's not the first time he'd looked that pissed off at a mess I'd gotten us into. And it certainly wouldn't be the last.

We hadn't been driving for five minutes when Dana reached into the glove compartment and pulled out a small plastic bag of pot, rolling a joint in her lap with practiced dexterity.

When you grow up in British Columbia, there's always pot around.[15] It wasn't like today, with dope smoking more socially acceptable than cigarette smoking, but nonetheless pot was always around in the shadows. I had smoked it myself, of course, and been around others who were smoking, but there was something about Dana and the way she rolled and lit that joint that was different.

In my experience, smoking a joint was either sacred or clandestine: you passed it around a circle,[16] or you toked deep and fast before you got caught.[17] Either way, there was nothing casual about it, and Dana was nothing if not casual. She smoked the joint like it was a cigarette, passing it occasionally to Dan. I was too stunned when he reached the joint back between the seats toward me to do anything but shake my head.

I glanced at Peter. His eyes were wide, with a clear message: "Do something!"

"Um...," I started. "Are you sure you should..."

"Oh yeah," Dan said, slowly. "I'm totally fine for driving."

"No, I mean... we're going into the U.S. and..."

Dana stared at me and Dan glanced back over his shoulder.

"We have to cross the border."

---

15. Especially if you're a music fan, with a habit of going to shows. On my first date with Shawna, my high school girlfriend, we went to a Bob Dylan/Tom Petty and the Heartbreakers show in 1986. When I was recounting this story to some friends years later, everyone nodded. "Oh, right. 1986. Summer of the Great Pot Drought." That's how deeply it runs in the culture: they remembered the Great Pot Drought before they remembered Expo 86.

16. One of my fondest memories is of being part of such a circle with a group of biker-stoners, watching a PBS special about NASA. But that's not my story to tell.

17. Or, if you were one of my friends, you adulterated your homemade cigarettes with weed, and took great delight in toking up in the smoking area between the main school and the industrial ed shops.

I don't know if you've spent much time with people who are smoking weed—and I suspect it's different now, especially in Canada, with the increased social and legal acceptance of marijuana[18] —but there are few things funnier than the moment when marijuana-induced paranoia comes head to head with an impending encounter with an authority figure.[19] Particularly an American authority figure. With a gun and a badge.

Dan and Dana went from chill to stoned freak-out mode in the space of less than a second. They both cranked their windows down as fast as they could, and Dana chucked the joint across Dan and out the driver's side. The baggie of weed went out her window, sailing toward the ditch as she began waving her hands, trying to fan out the skunky smoke. "Roll down your windows!" Dan shouted frantically from the front.

"My window's already down," Peter deadpanned, his hand still pressing the plastic firmly over the hole in the roof.

We did our best not to laugh.

We made it through the border without any hassles whatsoever, but Dan and Dana sulked all the way to Tacoma. They didn't even notice when Peter let go of the plastic and pulled his hand back into the car.

Thankfully, we weren't sitting with Dan and Dana, and the four of us split up when we got to the Tacoma Dome. Peter and I wandered around outside for a while, spending too much money on t-shirts, before we went inside and took our seats.

---

18. This was brought crashingly home to me a year or so ago. I was downtown, catching a bus back to work after a radio appearance. I was smoking a cigarette a good twenty feet from the nearest bus shelter. An elderly woman pushing a wire cart gave me the stink-eye all the way down the sidewalk and all the way into the shelter, where she sat down on the bench next to two nouveaux punks who were passing a joint back and forth. She smiled and talked to them for the several minutes before her bus arrived. I can only assume she came downtown that day to pick up some glaucoma medication. Nudge nudge, wink wink.

19. This statement is only true, however, if you are not high yourself. Speaking as someone who has flushed more than a couple of grams of weed down a toilet in his life, when you're high, there is nothing funny about this. Not a goddamn thing.

From the opening moments of the show, we were transfixed. The band entered one by one to the sound of a carnival waltz, buying tickets at a mock ticket-takers stand before taking their positions on stage and kicking into "Tunnel of Love." It was powerful and stirring at levels we didn't fully understand.

During the intermission, which followed a first set longer than most full rock concerts, we saw Dan and Dana walking determinedly toward us from wherever they had been sitting.

Dan shifted his weight uncomfortably from foot to foot as he said, "We're leaving." Dana looked smug and self-satisfied.

I couldn't believe what I was hearing. "What? How can you leave now?"

He shrugged. "We're just gonna go. Come on."

Peter and I were pretty much at Dan's mercy. We were two hundred miles from home and he had the car. We had next to no money, save what we had saved for our bus fare back to Agassiz from Vancouver the next morning.[20] We didn't have any choice but to follow him.

The thing is? It took you longer to read the above paragraph than it took me to say no. Far longer. I said no without even thinking about it.

Dan looked stunned.

Peter looked even more stunned.

"We're staying," I said.

Dan and Dana wandered away, shaking their heads. Peter stared at me. "How are we going to get home?"

"Fucked if I know," I said, as the lights went down for the second set.

There's lots I don't remember about that show, but the highlights stuck with me: "Roulette," the long-lost song Springsteen

---

20. The plan for our return to Agassiz was so convoluted I can't actually piece it together. As best as I can recall, Dan was supposed to drop us off at Sue's parents' (my step-grandparents') place in Surrey where we were going to crash for a few hours before getting a ride to the Skytrain to take it to go catch a bus from downtown Vancouver. Though I could be making all that up. I honestly have no idea.

wrote in the wake of the Three Mile Island incident; a raging "Light of Day" to close out the show; "Sweet Soul Music" in the encores; "Ain't Got You" blending seamlessly into "She's the One."

But there are two things I recall clearly.

The first was Bruce and Patti: the chemistry between them was palpable, even across the length of an arena. Constant eye contact, sultry expressions, an electric sense that anything could happen; Springsteen's marriage was clearly over.

The second was what happened in the encores. When Springsteen sang "Born to Run" in that stripped down, pleading, searching version, something broke inside me, cracking the walls I had built up around myself.

I was seventeen. I'd soon be leaving home. I was finishing school and going away, across the water to the University of Victoria. I had chosen UVic to put as much distance as I could between myself and everything I knew without getting on a plane.

I was terrified.

"Born to Run" had once inspired me to dream of blowing the dust and shit-smell from my little town off me as quickly as I could. But the reality had changed. I knew what I was running from, but what was I running to?

When I glanced over at Peter, as the song was ending, he looked devastated, sad and desperate, deeply uncertain and confused.

He looked like I felt.

The rest of the encores passed in a blur; they were designed to. Every Springsteen show has its own dynamic, but the plan seems to be the same: to wring every last bit of energy from the audience before releasing them into the night. I screamed myself raw, begging for just one more song.

Peter and I staggered out into the spring night, shredded by the concert but oddly subdued. That version of "Born to Run"... We were both carrying it with us.

And outside, we ran smack dab into our conundrum.

"So, how are we gonna get home?" Peter asked.

"I have no idea," I said, trying to see around the throngs of fans spilling out of the building.

"You have no—"

"Come on," I said, leading him through the crowd, up a hill into the parking lot.

I had seen the buses on the rise from the doors of the arena. A small army of near-identical charters, all with their engines running. Peter and I had to try two or three before we found one of the coaches that had been rented by CFOX for the night.

We threw ourselves on the mercy of the driver, recounting our tale of woe: the dope smoking, the poor condition of the car, and, perhaps most damningly, the decision to leave a Springsteen concert early.

After a quick consultation with a woman with a clipboard, the bus driver waved us aboard.

I was unconscious before the bus was even finished loading. The next thing I knew I was stumbling, sleep-clumsy, into a parking lot in downtown Vancouver at about three AM.

Peter and I walked for hours, not going anywhere because there was nowhere for us to go. We talked about the future, about what we figured was going to happen next for each of us. We talked about how excited we were, and how scared. We found an all-night restaurant, where we split an order of fries and gravy.

We sat in that restaurant as the sun came up. Nobody in the world knew where we were. Nobody was worrying about us. And we were fine.

It felt like what I had always imagined being a grown-up would feel like.

> Baby this town rips the bones from your back
> It's a death trap, it's a suicide rap
> We gotta get out while we're young
> 'Cause tramps like us, baby we were born to run

4th of July,
Asbury Park (Sandy)

Album: *The Wild, the Innocent & the E Street Shuffle*
Released: September 11, 1973
Recorded: June–August 1973

NOSTALGIA IS, by its very nature, bittersweet, the happiest memories laced with melancholy. It's that combination, that opposition of forces, that makes it so compelling. People, places, events, times: we miss them, and there's a pleasure in the missing and a sadness in the love.

The feeling is most acute, sometimes cripplingly so, when we find ourselves longing for the moment we're in, the people we're actually with.[1]

That nameless feeling, that sense of excruciating beauty, of pained happiness, is at the core of "4th of July, Asbury Park (Sandy)."

As a song, it's an impressionistic wonder, a kaleidoscopic portrait of the carnival life of the Asbury Park pier and beach in the late 1960s and early 1970s. The people in the song are as varied, and bizarre, as some of Dylan's characters, with the significant difference that some of these people are real: the Latin lovers and bikers and factory girls are types, but Madam Marie, for example, opened her fortune-telling parlor on the boardwalk in 1932 and didn't close it until 2008.

---

1. There should to be an English word for this feeling, but I haven't been able to find it. The Japanese call it *mono no aware*, "the pathos of things." Which, now that I think about it, would make a great tattoo.

The narrator is keenly aware of his time, their time, perhaps an epoch, passing, and he balances a wise acceptance with one last night of desperate resistance. He's lost his job, and his days of hanging on the boardwalk are coming to an end, but he's going to go down fighting. He also uses that sense of transience to make one last play for Sandy. You have to admire his moxie.

This is one of Springsteen's most gorgeous songs, and it captures that heady combination of joy and yearning. The arrangement is lush and romantic, both a complement and a counterpoint to the longing expressed in the lyrics.

The song, like the whole of *The Wild, the Innocent & the E Street Shuffle*, is firmly rooted in both personal experience and the changes in Springsteen's life. Recording once again at the miserable 914 Sound Studios, Springsteen's days of sleeping on the Asbury Park beaches by day and playing at night were behind him. He had a band to support, and a career to build: his carefree days were a thing of the past, and it's difficult not to hear that loss in "4th of July, Asbury Park (Sandy)."

Stepping back, it's also a powerful song on the social level. In 1970, part of downtown Asbury Park was destroyed by fires and race riots. This, after years of slow decline for the once-thriving beach destination. As Springsteen was writing the song, the town itself was dying.

My one reservation? This is going to sound persnickety, but I don't think it should be set on the Fourth of July. I understand the richness of context the date provides: the significance of the holiday, the fireworks, the crowds. But it doesn't work thematically or fit the narrative. The Fourth of July is almost the beginning of the summer. There are weeks of sun and sand and factory girls taking off their pants to come.

Surely the elegiac feeling of the song is more suited to Labor Day?

.   .   .

I HAVE A PROBLEM with people who can say, with a straight face, that their high school years were the best years of their lives. I have issues with high school being remembered as anything other than a trial by fire, but the assertion also makes me feel sad, in a strange way. Pitying, even. I want to ask, "If high school was the best part of your life, what have the last twenty years been? How does it feel to live like that, in a perpetual state of disappointment?" But I don't. I'm too polite.[2]

Greg and I have this conversation fairly often. He doesn't buy into the "high school as the best years" mindset, but he is a guy, it must be said, who left his small town to go to school in Vancouver, who moved to a different small town in the hinterland to get some seniority and experience, and then moved back to Agassiz at the earliest opportunity. He lives there still: as a homeowner, a doting father, and an administrator-teacher at the high school we attended.[3]

I can't wrap myself around spending much more than a weekend in Agassiz, let alone moving back there, but his experience of the town while growing up was vastly different from mine. He was an athlete, a star basketball player on the team that, in our senior year, won the Provincial Boys AA championship. He had an easy, casual way of being that seemed to allow any digs or teenage cruelty (usually directed at his height) to roll off him.

A lot of what makes his memories of high school so positive, though, are his friends. And on this I agree.

We were close, all of us. Kevin and Victor from the team. John, almost as big a Springsteen fan as Greg and I were. Brendan, a year younger than me but smarter and cooler and more confident and creative. The girls. Roseanne and Deanna and Karen. Nicole, who was at once my nemesis and competitor and a dear friend: we bickered like a couple from a 1940s romantic comedy. And Jennifer,

---

2. I'm not actually that polite. I just figure, why add to their pain?

3. That same high school now features a poster of me on their Wall of Fame. It was the first such poster, actually. I'm still working through the levels of irony and mental discord that fact creates in me. I should probably talk to someone. Perhaps on a couch.

with whom I was madly in love: a condition I never did anything about, not wanting to risk one of my great friendships.[4]

I had two girlfriends in the last few years of high school. Sisters, in fact.[5] I dated Andrea for a few months in the spring of 1986. We slow-danced to The Hooters in my family room while the opening ceremonies of Expo 86, the world's fair in Vancouver, played on the TV behind us.

At the time, Andrea's younger sister Shawna was one of my confidantes. She was pretty and sweet with a caustic sense of humor and a slight, charming insanity. I developed a huge crush on her, even as I was making out with her sister at any given opportunity.

When Andrea dumped me, I invited Shawna to the Bob Dylan/ Tom Petty and the Heartbreakers show in Vancouver. It was my second date ever. We kissed for the first time on the beach, a day or two later.[6] We were together for two years. And we spent a lot of that time at the beach.

The beach at Harrison was the focal point of my last few years in Agassiz. Beach-wise, it's nothing much—just a strip of sand and a man-made lagoon (which locals refer to as "the spit"[7]), with the miles of Harrison Lake stretching out postcard-perfect to the horizon. The main drag runs along the beach, and across the road is a string of hotels and motels and restaurants, anchored at one end by the "world-famous" Harrison Hotel (locals just call it The Hotel).

---

4. If I could give my sixteen-year-old self some advice, it would be this: make your move. Because that friendship you're trying so hard not to endanger? It doesn't turn out the way you think it will.

5. No, not at the same time.

6. The kiss probably wouldn't have happened were it not for a friend of my dad's named Larry. Upon seeing me mooning about the day after the show, he asked what was going on. When I told him the situation, how confused I was, how I didn't know if she even liked me, he shook his head. "Just kiss her," he said. "That's the only way you'll know for sure."

7. Given the temperatures the water reaches in summer (stagnant and cut off from the glacial chill of the lake) and the number of people in it, calling it "the spit" is more polite—though probably less accurate—than calling it "the lukewarm piss."

Also on the main drag was the Memorial Hall, an auditorium the size of a high school gym used for weddings, readings, concerts, and plays. Up a rickety set of stairs, well hidden save for a tiny window, was a room reserved for a couple of summers as the office for the Harrison Beach Patrol.

Greg and Shawna both worked for the Harrison Beach Patrol.

And they hated each other.

Greg thought Shawna was insane, and Shawna thought Greg was…well, Greg. I tried not to get in the middle, or to let it bother me.

The two of them working for the patrol wasn't the reason the beach became our main hangout, but it was a handy justification. We would spend whole days in the sand, lying on blankets, drinking beer or—more typically—wine coolers, which we could always get someone to bootleg for us from a bar near The Hotel. We'd hide the bottles from the police and the patrol under our blankets, unless the patrol was Greg, who kept his own bottle at the ready for his periodic stops.

When he wasn't working, Greg would bring his ghetto blaster, and we'd play Springsteen bootlegs or Tom Petty albums. Some of the stuff we played we called "woman-hating music," caught as we were in the throes of perpetual teenage heartbreak. We'd watch the city girls walking by in their bathing suits and t-shirts as we sipped our lukewarm booze. We'd walk around the spit, or swim across. We'd sleep in the sun.

Our gang was a loose, ever-changing constellation. People would come before work or after (or, in Greg and Shawna's cases, during). We'd sit for hours shooting the shit, making plans, making promises.

In the evenings we would convene at the home of whoever's parents were out or, failing that, whoever's basement rec room was the farthest from where their parents were.

We had what we thought were epic parties, complete with bootlegged booze and clandestine making out and, later, vomiting in flower beds. In retrospect, these parties were so innocent as to be adorable: an occasional joint might be smoked,[8] but there were no other drugs. No sex. No drinking and driving. No fistfights. We were practically wholesome, despite the images of ourselves that we had in our heads.

It was paradise, really. Every kid should have a summer or two like that.

And then it came to an end, like the credits rolling on a movie before it was really done. There was no gradual dissolution, not for me. For me, it stopped sharply on the Sunday of the Labor Day weekend, 1988.

Peter and Shawna had already left town before people started gathering at my house; they were headed—separately—for Edmonton: Peter to university, Shawna to stay with relatives while she did her grade twelve.

Despite the fact that my goodbye with Shawna had been considerably more intimate,[9] it was something that had happened with Peter a week or so prior that really stuck with me.

That last summer, Peter and I drove a lot. Well, he drove, commandeering his mother's car for things like Friday night trips into Vancouver for midnight showings of The Rocky Horror Picture Show. Some nights, late, after Shawna had gone home, we'd meet up and just drive. We'd often end up past Harrison, out of town, up the winding road to the provincial park at Green Point,[10] or farther, into the hills.

This was one of those nights. It was a Saturday, or early on a Sunday morning, and we were listening to the radio, not really talking,

---

8. Usually by me.

9. It's hard to tell whether it's just the rose-colored lenses of retrospect, or whether it really is the universe messing with your head, but have you ever noticed that the last time you make love with someone tends to be the best, the most fulfilling? I usually come down on the "universe messing with you" side of the argument: "Are you sure about this path? Are you really, really sure?" Mono no aware.

10. Green Point has a lot of memories for me. Family picnics. The day I almost drowned trying to impress that girl I mentioned previously. Nightswimming with a girl I was in love with, but would never tell.

as we rattled along a logging road. Van Morrison came on, singing "Moondance," and it was perfect: it was a cloudless night, the moon almost full, the air silver and end-of-summer cool. I turned up the music.

As we rounded the corner toward the wharf at Hicks Lake I think we both stopped breathing.

A low mist was clinging to the lake, and when the headlights hit it, it seemed solid, impenetrable.

We left the lights on as we got out of the car and walked down to the wharf.

I don't know what it was—maybe nothing more than angles and physics[11]—but the lights fell along the wharf with the brightness of daylight until they reached the last wooden slat. Beyond that, there was nothing but grey. Once we were down on the dock, there was nothing in the world but us, the short path ahead of us, and a swirling, silver-grey mystery beyond.

Everything I had been feeling since that spring, since hearing Springsteen sing "Born to Run" as that broken, melancholy ballad, came to a head. This was the end of things. Nothing in our lives would ever be the same. It was inevitable: within days, we were each going to be stepping off the end of that dock into the grey mystery, with no notion of whether we were going to drown or rise into the clouds.

I was shaking when we got back to the car.

We didn't talk about it, that night or ever. But it was clear, I think, that we had said goodbye not only to each other but to something inside ourselves.

That awareness made the party I hosted on the Sunday night of the Labor Day weekend both celebratory and sad.

It was great having (almost) everyone together, but our hedonistic enjoyment of the vodka and lemonade was undercut by the

---

11. Peter, who has become a physicist, would likely argue that there's never anything more than angles and physics.

knowledge that this was the last time our group would ever be together in the same way.

I wish I remembered more of that night; I got fairly drunk fairly early. I remember that Jennifer was beautiful in a pink summer dress. I remember all of us sitting in a circle on the carpet, drinking and telling stories. I remember Greg passing out on the couch, and Jennifer taking care of him.

I was sadder than I had ever been in my life to that point. And so happy I felt like I might just explode, fireworks over the town, over the lake, over my life.

I kissed Jennifer as she was leaving, and I remember the look she gave me, the sadness in her eyes, the love. It wasn't the first time we had kissed; it was the last time, though.

Sandy the aurora is risin' behind us
The pier lights our carnival life forever
Love me tonight for I may never see you again
Hey Sandy girl

Thundercrack

Album: *Tracks*
Released: November 10, 1998
Recorded: June 28, 1973

THIS WILL COME as no surprise to anyone who knows me: I'm not the world's most organized person. Quite the opposite, in fact. Some would argue that I'm a hoarder, though I haven't quite reached the stage where I might be featured on an exploitative television show.

This makes me, in many ways, a bad Tramp. I've got decades' worth of magazine articles, but do you think I can find them? My Springsteen books are scattered through a multitude of rooms in two separate buildings (three if you include the books still at my mom's place in Agassiz). My bootleg CDRs are mostly in unmarked sleeves in a box, labeled with a title and disc number if I'm lucky; no song listing, no dates, no other identifying information.

I tend to lose things. This was brought home to me—acutely—while writing this book. It wasn't just that it was a struggle to pull all the materials together. No, I even had trouble seeing things right in front of me.

Take "Thundercrack," for example.

One of the main reasons I was so thrilled when the *Tracks* box set came out in 1998 was that it contained—finally!—an official release of "Thundercrack." Sure, it was a studio recording, but beggars can't be choosers, right? I'd fallen in love with the song from bootlegs of legendary early seventies live shows, and I'd spent the last decade plus hoping that Springsteen Inc. might someday, in their infinite wisdom, release one of those live versions. I knew it was a vain hope; I knew there was no chance.

I knew that right up until I was writing the "Born to Run" chapter for this book.

I was watching the documentary included with the *Born to Run: 30th Anniversary* box set; I needed to confirm some information about the recording sessions, and the film is a gold mine.

And there, in the DVD menu?

"Thundercrack."

Not just a live version of the song, mind you. A live video, from 1973.[1]

Vintage.

It had been right there, under my nose, for five years, and I hadn't realized it.[2]

I can't express what a treasure this video is, a fossil record of what, at the time, was one of *the* Springsteen songs. It was everything I had envisioned, and more.[3] It's a balls-to-the-wall performance, filled with humor and intensity, superbly played and delivered with passion.[4]

Just another night in the bar for Springsteen and company.

---

1. The footage comes from a showcase gig that Springsteen and the band performed on May 1, 1973, at the Ahmanson Theatre in Los Angeles. They were third on a bill—one of the rare times Springsteen appeared as an opener after the disastrous Chicago tour, which also featured Doctor Hook & the Medicine Show and New Riders of the Purple Sage. The video is, like the "Rosalita" video, drawn from the original footage by Thom Zimny; sadly, it fades out at the ten minute point... (A confession: the main reason for this footnote is so my mom could be comforted by the knowledge that there was a time when Springsteen opened for Dr. Hook, her favorite band.)

2. Well, of course I had, at some point, realized I had it. I mean, I'm not an idiot. The presence of the three tracks from 1973 was obviously a selling point of the box set; I knew they were there. But, much like my 1992 copy of the *Musician* magazine interview, which I've been looking for for weeks... well, I lost sight of them.

3. The other two songs on the DVD, "Spirit in the Night" and "Wild Billy's Circus Story," are equally impressive, but for me it's all about "Thundercrack."

4. Springsteen has long claimed never to have done any drugs. It might just be my personal baggage, but performances like this one make me skeptical.

Even after the release of the first two albums, Bruce Springsteen and the E Street Band were journeymen musicians going from town to town, night after night, paying their dues. They played theatres and larger venues in cities where their following was developing (those cities—Philadelphia, New York, Boston—remain Springsteen hot spots to this day), but mostly their gigs were isolated, one-night barroom stands, winning their audience over one sweaty set at a time. You can follow the development of the band through what Springsteen once referred to[5] as "the magic of bootlegging."[6]

Two of the finest pre–*Born to Run* bootlegs were recorded at the Main Point, a bar in Bryn Mawr, Pennsylvania, two years apart.

The second show, on February 5, 1975, performed as a benefit for the club, finds the band on the cusp of their *Born to Run*–era powers. The almost three-hour set includes "Born to Run" itself and an early version of "Thunder Road" (with different lyrics, and under the title "Wings for Wheels"), along with definitive versions of "New York City Serenade" and, yes, "Incident on 57th Street."[7] The show also includes a carefully chosen set of covers, including "Mountain of Love," Chuck Berry's "Back in the U.S.A." as the show's finale, and a version of Bob Dylan's "I Want You" that has me weeping at the mere memory of it.

---

5. Over the course of his career, Springsteen has had a complex and often contradictory reaction to the idea of bootlegs. During radio broadcasts on the 1978 tour, he seemed to take a live-and-let-live approach (kicking off the second set of the July 5 show at the Roxy with the exultant encouragement "Bootleggers, roll your tapes! This is gonna be a hot one!"), yet he and his management were ruthless in their pursuit and prosecution of bootleg producers, distributors, and sellers. It's pretty much a moot point now, what with virtually every show appearing online almost as soon as Springsteen and the band leave the stage.

6. I would, of course, never encourage you to listen to bootlegs. Heavens no. Perish the thought.

7. I wore out my copy of *The Saint, the Incident and the Main Point Shuffle*, the bootleg of this show, listening to "Incident." It's a transcendent performance, utterly breathtaking, and here's the best part: it opens the fucking show. Yes, he opened the show with a song and a performance that it would be nearly impossible to top, then proceeded to top it, song after song.

If you're collecting Springsteen,[8] this show should be one of the cornerstones of your collection: it's damn near perfect.[9]

The earlier show, though, is actually more interesting, and just as strong. Recorded April 24, 1973, this show finds the band in their two-shows-a-night period. Their seven-song, hour-plus set was fairly standard in those days, and it includes an early version of "New York City Serenade" (entitled "New York City Song"), and a couple of tracks off the first album ("Spirit in the Night" and "Does This Bus Stop at 82nd Street," along with two of Springsteen's great, lost songs, "Santa Ana" and "Tokyo" (aka "And the Band Played").[10] When we first got that bootleg, Greg and I spent hours, days, poring over the words, building the story up in our mind.

The set finished, as sets did in those days, with "Thundercrack."

"Thundercrack" was the showstopper. It's flat-out rock and roll, soul-infused, with sing-along spots, call and response, and plenty of room for soloing and schtick. In the earlier Main Point show, it's thirteen minutes of rock-and-roll baptism; like "Rosalita" would be in years to come, it's pure, undistilled joy.

And it's all about a girl who likes to dance.

LEAVING HOME at seventeen to go to university on Vancouver Island was the best thing I could have done. I knew that by the middle of my first year. No baby steps for me; no living at home while I did a year or two at Fraser Valley College. No schools on the mainland, where I could easily go home for weekends. I wanted the hour and a half on the ferry, that stretch of open water between me and my past.

---

8. I would, of course, never encourage you to collect bootlegs. Heavens no. Perish the thought.

9. I added that "damn near" under duress, and due to not wanting to look like a complete geek. I'll correct it here: it's a perfect show, and the bootleg would be one of my ten desert island discs, no question.

10. "Santa Ana" was eventually released on *Tracks*, but nothing rivals the one-two punch of these songs in the early Springsteen sets.

On Labor Day 1988, though, I couldn't shake the feeling that it was the worst idea I had ever had.

My mother borrowed her boyfriend's car, a sporty little number, to get me to Victoria. I moved to university with less stuff than it took to fill the trunk of the z28: a few books, my tapes, and my clothes. Included in the latter were fourteen identical pairs of robin's-egg blue underwear.

Two weeks earlier, after one last bout of back-to-school shopping for me, my mother had come home from Chilliwack very proud. She had bought me fourteen pairs of identical white socks, and the fourteen pairs of underwear. "There's enough for two weeks, and this way you never have to worry about socks not matching."

I was transfixed by the blue underwear. "Blue?"

"This way you won't mix them up with anyone else's laundry."

It was sound in principle, but I knew that it was a recipe for disaster. (Which would hit, less than a month later, when I returned to my building's laundry room to fetch my load out of the dryer and found the heartbreakingly beautiful Ukrainian exchange student who lived on the fourth floor in the final stages of folding my clothes. Right there, as if a spotlight was shining on them, a teetering stack of carefully folded powder blue underwear. Thirteen pairs. I was wearing the other. I was never able to look her in the eye again.)

My mother woke me up at four that Labor Day morning—I'd been asleep for about an hour. I slept in the car on the way to the ferry.

A few hours later, she dropped me off at my room, Helmcken 211.

I don't know what I was expecting from a university residence, but the Lansdowne complex wasn't it. The six buildings of the complex were identical, squat grey structures roughly the shape of cinder blocks. And about as welcoming. Everything was concrete, brutalist. The quad between the buildings was off-kilter, as if the six cinder blocks had been kicked out of true and left where they landed. Later in the fall, when the rains of October and November hit, I'd discover that the buildings seemed to bleed, with streaks of wet black against the grey like open wounds.[11]

It was only when my mother was gone that I realized what "alone" really meant.

The thing with growing up in a place like Agassiz, living there for your whole life, is that you know everyone. I had a hard enough time making friends, but I didn't have to worry about actually *meeting* people for the first time.

And then there I was, hours from home, completely alone, and with absolutely no idea what to do. Once again, I was the little kid in the big school with the big kids, and me with nothing to offer.

I had a roommate, but he came with his own set of friends; I had left mine behind. There was one guy I knew slightly already, Dave, and we hung out some. He'd eventually trade spots with my roommate, but for the first few weeks I felt utterly, inconsolably alone.

I wasn't prepared for it. I had envisioned meeting people immediately, striking friendships that would last a lifetime, falling into a period of shameless promiscuity. Instead, I spent most of my time in class, reading old record reviews from *Rolling Stone* off the microfiche in the library basement, or sitting on the window ledge of my room, watching people coming and going.

It was the fall of Guns N' Roses' *Appetite for Destruction*. Every Friday night people would put their speakers on their windowsills and "Welcome to the Jungle" would echo through the concrete quad. Cases of beer and forties of booze were set up in party rooms or carried from scene to scene.

I was paralyzed. I had always known that I was an outsider, an onlooker, a misfit, but I hadn't realized just how shy I was. When I went to parties, I would end up standing back near the wall, unable to bring myself to talk to anyone. It was easier to just not go.

So I threw myself into swimming and movies.

---

11. It was a terrible place to warehouse hundreds of hormonal, scared seventeen- and eighteen-year-olds. We used to hear stories of undergrads who "dove a stairwell," attempting suicide, and I always wondered why more people didn't do it.

UVic, then and now, had a fantastic film society, with a different movie—often a double feature—screening at the Cinecenta in the student union building every night. I went to everything in those early days: documentaries, foreign films, blockbusters on the weekends, and midnight showings of cult favorites. I was there five nights a week, ensconced in my preferred seat dead center in the second row. I'd fill the time before the movie, or in the break between halves of a double feature, scrawling in one of a series of black notebooks that I always carried with me.

The other two evenings of each week I took my lifeguard training. I had been working at the pool in Agassiz for a couple of summers, but it was time to recertify, so I signed up for a class that ran Tuesdays and Thursdays at the campus pool. The demands of the program forced me to swim every night. I'd go to a movie with my bag containing swimsuit, towel, and goggles in hand and head to the pool as soon as the lights came up. Within a couple of weeks I was swimming ten kilometers a night.

Which is how I found myself, on the third Saturday in September, exhausted and spent and flying from endorphins, staggering back to my room.

Second Helmcken. Second door on the right.

I didn't want to be alone that night. The third weekend in September was the annual Agassiz Fall Fair, the high-water mark of the year for my little town. It was the archetypal country fair, with a midway, and rides, and a craft competition, and the judging of everything from apples to livestock. The barns were always packed, everyone milling past cows and sheep and roosters and rabbits. Most years, four of my mother's siblings turned up for the fair, and occasionally the full set of seven Eddys would congregate around the table at my grandmother's for dinner.

All of a sudden I was one of those Island relatives, cut off by the strait. All of a sudden all that distance that I had fought so hard for seemed like a really bad idea. I was lonesome, and a long way from home.

I tossed my swim stuff into my room and did something I had never done: I went to the lounge between the second and third floors.

There were three people in the small room: two girls who were just leaving, dressed for a party, and a girl sitting astride the padded bench closest to the TV, which was playing the Miss America Pageant.

I took a place on the couch—about as far as I could get from the girl on the bench and still be in the same room—and tried to watch the show.

The girl on the bench was beautiful. Long dark hair, in curls, falling to the top of her back. Brown eyes. Glasses. A gorgeous smile. Shapely.

But what drew my eye was that she never stopped moving. It wasn't hyperactivity, just a sense of barely contained momentum. She was like quicksilver, the way it never seems to rest, the way it shimmers, the way it shines.

Then she asked if I had been swimming. Her voice in the otherwise empty room startled me. After the previous few weeks, I was getting used to invisibility.

I suspect I stammered. I suspect that in the long history of opening lines, mine was well toward the bottom of the ranking.

And then she asked if she could brush my hair.

What would you have done?

I raced down to my room and returned in seconds with my hairbrush, sure that she would be gone by the time I got back.

But she wasn't.

She shimmied back on the bench, leaving me room in front of her.

We talked as she brushed my long hair. She was gentle. Never pulled. We mocked the pageant, and I told her about the fall fair, and asked about her classes, and she told me about where she grew up, and when she handed me back the hairbrush, she said, "I'm Cori."

We spent hours that night parceling out tiny bits of ourselves, devouring what we were offered. When she told me that she had been a dancer, that she had done jazz and ballet until her knees went, everything made sense. A line had been going through my head since I first saw her, that sinuous, endless movement.

"She's got the heart of a ballerina."[12]

Cori and I became friends after that. One of the guys on my floor had a ridiculous crush on her, and she was spending a lot of time in his room down the hall, so I started gravitating that way as well. We'd hang out, talking about Monty Python, throwing darts, each of us trying to show the other up. Cori was dating a guy I had an English class with. And I befriended her next-door neighbor, two floors up.

Being friends with Cori, pursuing her in my clumsy, inexperienced way, forced me out of myself. I had to socialize, if I wanted to be around her. Which came with its own cost.

There weren't many nights I was sober between that October and the following February.[13]

One of the nights I was, I met up with Cori in the lounge after my swim. It was mid-October, and I brought my hairbrush.

We spent most of the night sitting there, watching MuchMusic. This was back when the station still showed videos, including a new U2 song ("Desire"), and a live video for Springsteen's "Tougher Than the Rest" that had been shot a couple of days before the show Peter and I went to in Tacoma.

We stayed up till three or four, talking and laughing, pressed close on the couch, waiting for those songs. And after we had seen both, neither of us wanted to leave.

---

12. All of "Thundercrack" reminds me of Cori, not just because of how much she loves to dance, but because the lyrics get her so hilariously, directly wrong: she does have curls, her hair is brown (or was then), and her eyes are too. It makes me smile every time I hear the song.

13. I would like to be able to claim that, as I've matured, I've gotten better, both with the social anxiety and with limiting my alcohol consumption. Can we pretend, for the sake of argument, that this is true?

That was when I knew there was something. I wasn't sure what, but something.

Cori's suitor, my floor brother, was still in hot pursuit, and as Halloween approached, he ramped things up drastically: he asked her to a movie. A Friday midnight horror movie at Cinecenta, something from the *Nightmare on Elm Street* oeuvre, if memory serves.

In response, I asked Cori's neighbor to the movie. She surprisingly upped the ante, suggesting—no, stating outright—that after the movie I could spend the night with her.

The four of us went off, a happy little incestuous ménage. We watched the movie, and we walked back to our building. Cori disappeared into the room at the end of the hall, and my date went upstairs first. I want to say that she used the phrase "slip into something more comfortable," but that can't possibly be true.

I went to brush my teeth. And when I came back from the bathroom, vibrating with thoughts of the night ahead (at last, all the collegiate sex I had been expecting was going to happen!), Cori was waiting in my room.

I never did make it upstairs.[14]

We lay on my bed, talking. That was it. At about four, we crawled under the covers, and held each other as we went to sleep.

That's the night we consider our anniversary.

The next night was the Halloween dance, which coincided[15] with a floor crawl hosted by our sister floor, fourth Ravenhill. If you haven't experienced a floor crawl, picture twelve residence rooms, all with their doors open. Picture each room with a different drink for its guests, ranging from the banal (Lucky Lager, official beer of Vancouver Island) to the ridiculous.

The latter, that night, was a yukaflux. That spelling might be wrong, but it doesn't really matter. It's the principle that counts:

---

14. I had never asked her, outright, so I asked Cori tonight if she did it on purpose, if she had cockblocked with intent. Tonight, twenty-two years later, she smiled. "Of course not," she lied.

15. Not coincidentally.

sliced fruit by the pound soaked in a cooler full of overproof liquor, a near-toxic stew of vodka, rum, gin, whatever these underage girls could get their hands on. Topped off, just before the guests arrived, with champagne and fruit juice.

The drink was effective enough. It was the fruit that killed me.

Cori and I had decided, over breakfast that morning, that we would go to the dance that night. It wasn't a date, it was a foregone conclusion, really, considering.

By the time we got to the dance, though, I could barely walk. I certainly couldn't see. I remember talking to Cori the next day, telling her what a fantastic time I had had, how I couldn't believe that they had played Neil Young's "Cinnamon Girl" so often.

"They didn't play it at all," she said.

"But...I must have danced to it, like, fifty times."

"That," she deadpanned, "explains a lot."

It was one of those nights where memory is shaky at best.

I do remember one moment, though: leaning in to her on the dance floor, fearlessly, and kissing her for the first time.

I remember it like it was yesterday.[16]

And I remember, with the same clarity, another moment from another drunken night, about a month later.

This time, Cori came to my rescue.

The party was in my room, a quiet, sedate affair of twenty or twenty-five young adults crammed into a room no larger than your average prison cell. I was flying high, top of the world, and then I rubbed my eyes and dislodged a contact, which proceeded to bury itself under the curve of my eyeball.

I stumbled out of the room, half blind, into the brightness of the washroom. And Cori followed. She found me there, yarding my eyelids open in front of the mirror, fingers thick with drink, trying to figure out what the hell I was going to do.

---

16. So does she, apparently. We were talking about it yesterday. Telling Xander the story. Apparently I was clumsy, and practically falling over, and a little slobbery. And she was smiling as she told him all about it.

She sat me down on the counter, and told me to lean back my head and open my eyes.

And as she gently dipped the tip of her pointer finger toward my eye, I whispered, "I love you."

I don't know where it came from. I wasn't planning on saying it. But I knew, in that moment, trusting her enough to want her to stick a finger in my eye, that I could trust her with anything.

She stopped, and looked at me, and smiled, and said "I love you too."

And then, without hesitation, she slid her finger into my eye and popped out my contact lens, and we kissed, and held each other, both of us knowing that our lives had changed, right then.

She moves up, she moves back
Out on the floor there just is no one cleaner
She does this thing she calls the "Jump back Jack"
She's got the heart of a ballerina

Side Two

Yeah, I know I ain't nobody's bargain
But, hell, a little touchup
and a little paint…
BRUCE SPRINGSTEEN, "Human Touch"

Tunnel of Love

Album: *Tunnel of Love*
Released: October 9, 1987
Recorded: January–July 1987

ONE OF THE secrets of a good mix-tape lies in the recognition that you're dealing with two separate entities, each with its own concerns, but each working in tandem with the other.[1] Each side of the tape should tell its own story, develop its own themes and movement. Sometimes the two sides build off one another (this is useful for mix-tapes intended for wooing). Other times, the two sides will create a contrast. Light and dark, happy and sad, that sort of thing.

It's appropriate for both my life and Springsteen's that the tape flip here happens with "Tunnel of Love."

It's pretty clear that the *Tunnel of Love* album was a turning point for Springsteen. Prior to *Tunnel*, Springsteen's work was largely external to himself. From the doomed greasers of "Jungleland" to the blue collar workers of "Factory" to the disenfranchised Vietnam veteran of "Born in the U.S.A.," the songs were clearly and deliberately stories. Until then, Springsteen dealt in emotional veracity without treading too close to personal emotional truth.

With *Tunnel of Love*, however, he changed tack. Yes, there were

---

1. Sort of like a marriage, that. Just in case the metaphor was too gentle.

still story-songs (Springsteen has never been a desperate single mother trying to decide not to drown her young son in a river, as the heroine of "Spare Parts" finds herself doing), but there were also songs that seemed, at least, to come directly from his own experience.[2] Given the albums that followed, it's easy to see *Tunnel of Love* as the moment that Springsteen began to turn inward, exploring himself at least as much as he was exploring the lives of the people around him.

He chose a hell of a place to start.

Upon its release in 1987, *Tunnel of Love* was regarded as his marriage album, his first collection of new material since marrying Julianne Phillips during the *Born in the U.S.A.* tour. It is not, however, an account of a man growing fat and happy in his new domestic kingdom. Steeped in betrayal, pain, and recrimination, *Tunnel of Love* has more in common with the emotional brutality of Bob Dylan's *Blood on the Tracks* than it does with the comforting homilies of Crosby, Stills and Nash's "Our House." Just the song titles alone—"Ain't Got You," "Cautious Man," "Two Faces," "Brilliant Disguise," "When You're Alone"—alert even the casual listener that all was not well in Casa Springsteen.

Tunnel of Love also marked a shift in Springsteen's process. He recorded the album's basic tracks largely on his own, bringing in band members only as necessary for texture and flourish. The Bo Diddley–esque opener, "Ain't Got You," is a Springsteen solo track, and The E Street Band appears together only on the title song. Clarence Clemons, whose saxophone had been key to Springsteen's sound, is relegated to a single appearance on the record, as a background vocalist on "When You're Alone."

We'll never know how closely the songs on *Tunnel of Love* hew to

---

2. Emphasis must be placed on the word "seem." We have no way of knowing, for example, if the account of the relationship between father and son in "Walk Like a Man" is rooted directly in Springsteen's personal experience. But we do know about the fraught-at-times relationship he had with his father, so it's easy (and, given his use of the first-person narrative voice, fairly compelling) to speculate.

the disintegration of Springsteen's own marriage, or to the reality of his doubts and questions.

We do know this, though: in the liner notes, he writes, "Thanks Juli."

CORI AND I got married in the side yard of my mother's house on the Saturday of a May long weekend. May 16, 1992. It was a beautiful afternoon, sunny but not overly warm. We had a few friends there, but it was mostly a family affair.

In my family, we do up large-scale occasions with a practiced ease. Christmas dinners for thirty are old hat. Family reunions are even easier, with their potluck nature. For the wedding, my grandmother cooked and my aunts brought food. My dad and Sue supplied the booze. And Jon spent the morning wandering the country roads, stopping in at houses with gardens to ask for flowers.[3]

Cori was carrying a basket of flowers as she walked toward me, up the front walk and across the grass, to the sound of Van Morrison's "Tupelo Honey." She really was, as Van sang, "an angel of the first degree." Her mother had made the dress, and I had a piece of the same ribbon tying back my ponytail.

Peter was in Germany, on a family trip that couldn't be changed. Greg was there, though, with Lisa, the woman he would marry a year later in a splendid extravaganza in Vancouver. Our friend Dorothy, who was in classes with Cori, served as her maid of honor. In the card she gave us, Dorothy confessed to being relieved that we were finally married: with her strict Catholic background and

---

3. Jon is very polite, and very good with people, especially people with gardens. He brought home basketfuls of flowers.

"People just gave you these?" I asked, incredulous.

"Most of them," he said, cutting stems over the sink.

"What do you mean, most of them?"

"Well, if somebody's gonna be an asshole, they don't deserve to have such pretty flowers, do they?"

It took a moment for it to sink in. "You committed misdemeanors for décor?"

He patted me on the cheek. "It's your wedding day, big brother. Of course I did."

beliefs, she had feared for our mortal souls due to our premarital transgressions.

Cori and I had moved in together at the beginning of our second year at UVic. We had planned on sharing a house with a bunch of people, but things fell through, and it ended up just the two of us in a shitty, furnished ground-level apartment.

By the time we got married, we were living in an attic suite over a daycare. Every Saturday night we had a houseful of people over, a loose circle of friends gathering to watch the weekly double-header of *Star Trek: The Next Generation* and *Deep Space Nine*. We both worked while we were going to school, so those Saturday night get-togethers were our only social life, populated as they were with people we knew from our classes, co-workers from my job at the bookstore or hers at the community center. The kitchen was downstairs, part of the daycare. We would make a big pot of soup over the course of the day and bake some soda bread to go along with it once people had arrived. The evenings would usually dwindle to a finish sometime after the end of *Saturday Night Live*.[4]

Cori and I were the picture of responsibility in those years. We both worked all through our degrees to avoid onerous student loans. Aside from a couple of nights in Vancouver, we skipped our honeymoon so we wouldn't miss work.[5]

We traveled a little bit (though we never made it to Europe as planned), and we got into the habit of going to New York as often as we could.

As our friends started to leave town after they finished their degrees, we grew closer. Our Saturday nights turned into games nights, playing Scrabble or Monopoly, eating cookies and drinking tea.

---

4. That ritual viewing of SNL was not without its risks. Dorothy was fine with bawdy, frat-boy humor, but we were watching the night that Irish singer Sinead O'Connor tore up a photograph of the Pope while crying out "Fight the real enemy!" as the climax to her cover of Bob Marley's "War." Dorothy's reaction was … intense, to say the least.

5. A decision we now both regret, though it made sense at the time.

It was a good life. Comfortable.

And we bought a house.

Oh, the house.

After a fairly lengthy search in Victoria and its neighboring communities, we found a house close to downtown, a 1910 home that had been in the same family for most of its eight-decade history. We bought it from a couple with two kids. It felt homey, but we also bought the house with the idea of tearing it down, sundering the conjoined double lot, and building two skinny houses. That was our medium-term plan, a way of having a new house for the cost of an old one.

It was an old house. We didn't imagine being in it any more than five years.

Fourteen years later, it's an even older house. It's riddled with problems (right now, there's no heat or hot water, and a mysterious amount of water in the basement). These days, the only thing holding it together is debt.

That's the way these things go sometimes.

The old expression, that man plans and God laughs? That's pretty much spot on.[6] There's supposed to be a natural order of things, isn't there? It's like a checklist: you leave home, you go to school, you fall in love, you get a job, you get married, you buy a house—that's how it's supposed to work.

But it doesn't, always.

You don't realize, as you're struggling to balance work and school, sacrificing on both sides, that you're going to get fired at the first sign of problems, and you'll find that the degree you busted your ass to earn isn't worth much of anything.

You don't realize, walking through a cozy family home, holding hands with your wife, that someday you're going to be up to your knees together in a sewage-flooded basement, or you'll be holding a ladder for her when she goes up to tar patch the roof. Again. That

---

6. Though it's certainly open to agnostic, atheistic, or interfaith diddling. I'm partial to "man plans, and the universe mocks," because that's how it feels some days.

things will get so bad your home feels like a prison you just can't escape.

You don't realize as you're kissing your wife for the first time that there will be days when you're no longer two people fighting against the world, but two people fighting against each other, or that things you were once so sure of would become riddled with doubt.

And you don't realize, standing in the yard of the house you grew up in on a lovely warm spring day, watching the most beautiful girl in the world walk toward you on her father's arm, that the road ahead of you is bumpier, and more fraught with peril, than you can possibly imagine.

Those are things you have to find out the hard way.

That's why the Tunnel of Love rides in old amusement parks have that warning sign, just as you're about to go in: "This Is a Dark Ride."

It ought to be easy ought to be simple enough
Man meets woman and they fall in love
But the house is haunted and the ride gets rough
And you've got to learn to live with what you can't rise above

Living Proof

Album: *Lucky Town*
Released: March 31, 1992
Recorded: September 1991–January 1992

LOST SIGHT OF Springsteen for a while there, from about the time Cori and I moved in together up to the reunion tour of 1999–2000. A decade or so.

I use the term "lost sight" in a relative sense: I bought the three new studio albums that he released during that time. I bought the import edition of the *xxPlugged* CD, and the *Tracks* box set. I followed newsgroups and listservs on that new interweb thing that everyone was talking about. I was, even in what I think of as my disconnected years, what most normal people would consider a zealot.

It didn't feel that way to me, though. In the throes of finishing my degree,[1] working full-time, and starting married life, Springsteen wasn't speaking to me in the same way any more. He wasn't important.

I liked the records, but it didn't go much beyond that. Greg still has, in his collection, an unused ticket from a show at the Tacoma Dome in the early nineties that was supposed to be mine—he mocks me with it about once a year. I regret not going, and I kick

---

1. I wrote the graduating thesis for my Honors undergrad on linguistic variations in Bob Dylan's "Tangled Up in Blue"—Cori has yet to forgive me for the three months of constant Dylan (eight or nine versions of the song!) she had to endure.

myself, to this day, for not going to one of the solo acoustic theatre shows on the *Ghost of Tom Joad* tour, but at the time it didn't really seem to matter all that much.

Looking back, I can see I was in an in-between space as far as Springsteen's music was concerned. I had outgrown the youthful anthems of escape, and I was too contented then to connect with the post-therapy albums *Human Touch* and *Lucky Town*, released on the same day in 1992.

That changed, though.

Now those two albums, with their songs of deep soul-searching, speak to me more directly than any Springsteen work before or since.[2] They are albums of hard-won domestic happiness, with just enough self-effacing humor—in songs like "57 Channels (And Nothing On)" and "Local Hero"—to keep them from being nauseatingly saccharine.[3]

As I mentioned earlier, Springsteen found happiness in the arms of his longtime back-up singer, Patti Scialfa, after the breakup of his first marriage. They married in 1991, when Patti was pregnant with their second child, their daughter, Jessica. (Their eldest, son Evan, was born a year earlier.) Rumors about his divorce—which was sealed up tight in apparently bulletproof nondisclosure agreements—claimed that one of the reasons for Springsteen's unhappiness with Phillips was that he wanted a family, and she

---

2. These are among Springsteen's less popular albums. Some fans resented his firing of The E Street Band, and their fondness for Springsteen flagged as a result. More significantly, though, these are two of Springsteen's weakest albums. Unlike *Born to Run* or *Darkness*, on which every track was a classic, these albums contained a fair bit of filler ("Roll of the Dice," anyone? "Man's Job"?). Fans actually created a single-disc compilation of the best tracks off the two albums, referred to either as *Lucky Touch* or *Human Town*.

3. Speaking of saccharine, though? One of my favorite songs on *Human Touch* is the closing track, "Pony Boy." A gentle ballad, it's a lullaby for Springsteen's oldest son Evan, but it also serves as a wonderful resolution for many of the album's themes. It does, however, galvanize the fans. I may be the only person who likes it. That's fine, though. They can keep "Hungry Heart"; I'll take this one.

wanted to focus on her acting career. Whether this is true or not, by the time of the albums' release, Springsteen was the father of two, resettled in California.

Springsteen worked painstakingly on *Human Touch* over a period of about a year, recording in concentrated bursts with a group of Los Angeles session musicians. The album was ostensibly finished in early 1991, but Springsteen felt he needed one more song. Instead, he wrote and recorded an entire second album in a matter of weeks at his home studio, then decided to release both records on the same day.

The first song he wrote for *Lucky Town*, the bridge between the two albums, is "Living Proof."

The song chronicles the building of a family from the ashes of Springsteen's personal struggles, his negativity and despair. It's definitely post-therapeutic, and it marks the next stage in the story, his hard-won "close band of happy thieves," after *Tunnel of Love*'s relentless questioning and the very personal tests of *Human Touch*. It's profound and stirring.

And it starts on a summer afternoon, with the birth of a child.

THE CLAIM borders on cliché: "The only pain worse than a kidney stone is labor."

That assertion is also fundamentally wrong. I don't have first-hand experience, lacking both calcium buildups and ovaries, but I've seen both in action. I've held the monitoring strip in my hand.

That's jumping ahead, though. We need to go back a year or two from August 26, 1999, for the context.

Cori and I knew from the beginning that we were going to be parents. But it was a matter of timing. We had a pregnancy scare early on—midway through our second year at UVic—and after that we were very careful. We wanted everything to be just perfect: we wanted to have our degrees behind us, own a house, have steady jobs if not actual careers. We wanted everything to be as stable as possible before we had kids.

When we hit that point, we started trying.

Anyone who's had a scare can tell you how easy it is to get pregnant. But until you're actually trying you don't know just how tough it can be.[4] A few months went by. Months of furious and frequent lovemaking, of cautiously raised hopes and cyclical disappointment.

We did everything right. Not only did Cori eat better, and eliminate potential trouble areas like caffeine, but I, concerned about my contribution,[5] started exercising, cleaned up my diet, and cut out coffee, alcohol, and my couple-of-times-a-week cigars. No sacrifice was too great.

And we kept trying.[6]

I took a break on my birthday, November 25, 1998. I'd booked the day off work, and when I woke up I pressed myself a carafe of coffee that, after months without, tasted like heaven. I sat out on the front porch all day, drinking gin and tonics and smoking cigars. Cori and I went out for dinner to celebrate, breaking every single one of our self-imposed rules.

A little less than a month later, Cori gave me an early Christmas present: a calendar for 1999. It took me a while to notice that she had marked a page in mid-August with a tiny strip of thick paper with a blue stripe at one end.

When I looked at her, not really believing what I was seeing, she smiled. "I washed it," she said. "And dried it carefully."

---

4. If you've read my novel *Before I Wake*, this might sound familiar: the deliberateness of Cori's and my timing, and the resulting attempts, is the source of Simon and Karen's experience of conception in that book. Simon and Karen struggled for years, though— for Cori and me it was only a few months.

5. I'm not comfortable using the phrase "daily sperm production" even in a footnote, but yeah, that.

6. Everyone knew we were trying. I recall a weekend at Cori's folks' place, sitting down to breakfast with Rolf and June. My father-in-law asked, good-naturedly, how things were going. When I replied that we were trying, he suggested that I should be trying harder. "Well," I said, reaching for the butter, "I was trying a few minutes ago. I thought I'd get some breakfast before I try again." I don't recall him asking again after that.

Cori had a great pregnancy. We walked to work together every day, and went to prenatal classes, and decorated the baby's room. She was never sick, her energy was high, she hit or exceeded every milestone.

It's no wonder the baby didn't want to leave.

Her due date came and went, without a sign of a contraction. The baby was big, and content to remain within. A day passed. A week.

Nothing happened.

Finally, ten days past the due date, we went to a doctor's appointment at the hospital. Cori's fluid volume was low, and it was time to induce. That was the twenty-fifth of August.

We got her checked into the hospital, got her comfortable, and they gave her an injection of oxytocin to induce labor.

Nothing happened.

I stayed with her until visiting hours were over. We were waiting for a sign. We were waiting for our new life to start. It was right there, so close we could almost see it.

And nothing happened.

I went home alone. After calling her parents and mine, I sat out on the porch with a cigar and a bourbon and the cordless phone. It didn't ring.

I found out the next morning, when I arrived at the hospital shortly past dawn, that her water had broken, and the first of the contractions had hit at about three AM. Nothing more than twinges, though. No reason to wake me up.

Things started happening around ten with the first major contraction. Moments later the kidney stone, disturbed from whatever precarious perch it had been painlessly occupying, lodged itself painfully and undeniably smack in the middle of our birth story.

Cori vaulted out of the bed, stumbling in blind pain toward the bathroom. She almost made it, but she ended up barfing in the sink.

The rest of the day unfolds like a battle: shards of memory and confusion.

I remember sitting at the edge of the bed, Cori hooked up to equipment to monitor the strength of her contractions, watching as each wave of pain hit and peaked and passed, completely unnoticed by Cori, who was sweating and borderline delirious from the kidney stone pain.

I remember arguing with the nurses, none of whom believed that Cori was having a kidney stone episode, ascribing the situation with derisive glances and clucking of tongues to another first-time mother not being prepared.

I remember being told, over and over again, to wait for the doctor, who would decide if a specialist should be called in. And when would the doctor be there? "Later," they said. I have never felt more violent toward a group of women in my life. Didn't they see what was going on?

Finally a doctor coming in, a stranger. He took one look at Cori and asked, "You've had kidney stones before?"

She nodded and gasped, "Yes."

"Right. Then you know exactly what this is. Nurse?" The nurse leapt to attention.

The next hour or so exists only in fragments. Watching Cori get an epidural, turning away as the needle slipped into her lower back. An assessment, with stirrups, and a quick decision that, no, this wasn't going to happen on its own. The rush to an operating theatre. Scrubbing up. Putting on surgical greens.

And then I was at the head of Cori's bed, perched on a stool behind the wires and tubes, stroking her forehead as the anesthetic rushed into her.

The one thing the doctor told me, our doctor, who had finally arrived, was "Don't look over the curtain." He pointed at the institutional green sheet drawn up taut as a trampoline between Cori's head and the rest of her body. I kept hunched low, watching Cori breathe, listening to the doctors and nurses joke casually back and forth about their weekends as they cut into my wife's body.

An endless moment seemed to hang in suspension, a moment I feel like I've never truly escaped.

And then our doctor, Doctor Dave, said, "It's a boy."

I almost wept.

"Do you have a name?"

"Alexander," I said, without hesitation. "Alexander James."

I don't know where it came from.[7] I don't know why it burst out of my mouth so fully formed. Cori and I had a list of possible names for boys and girls, and Alexander James was nowhere on it. James was my grandfather's name, and there were several Jameses and Jims in the generations since, so we hadn't even considered it.

And yet...

Alexander James. Xander.[8]

It stuck.

"Do you want to see him?"

I'm not good with kids. I don't know how to hold them, or what to do if they cry. Xander was crying, but there was nothing I wanted more, right then, than to see him and hold him.

The anesthetist lifted the wild nest of tubes and cables and gestured for me to go under. I dropped to my knees from the stool and crawled.

But I made a mistake, like Orpheus at the gates of Hades. I looked to my left. I looked under the table.

I had never seen anything so horrific in my life. It looked like a MASH unit, drenched in blood and—

I turned my head and kept crawling until the operating table was behind me, until I could risk standing up without seeing anything else.

And there was our son. My son.

He was beautiful, and perfect, and crying. And as I watched, he peed on the nurse who was lowering him to the warming tray.

---

7. This, it turns out, is not entirely true. I've been reminded that early on in our relationship, I bought Cori a teddy bear, which she named Alexander James Fuzzy Wuzzy Skadoodle Bear. I make no further comment, except, "Huh. Weird."

8. At the reunion of our prenatal class a few months later we were stunned to find that of the thirteen babies born, nine had been named some variation of Alexander (including several Alexandras). Calling him Xander was a way of making him distinct, and avoiding people calling him Alex. (One has to wonder, though—were there that many teddy bears making the rounds, or was there something in the air?)

His first order of business upon arriving in the world had been to piss on an authority figure.

My boy.

The nurse picked up a set of surgical scissors and extended them toward me. "Do you want to cut the cord?"

I looked down at Xander's belly, at the tube of flesh, and I blanched. Cutting the cord felt important. Decisive. Significant. But I couldn't do it.

I shook my head.

As the nurse lowered the scissors to the umbilical cord, I flinched and looked away.

That meant I was looking directly at the table. Directly back at Cori.

It was ... terrible.

I knew, rationally, what a C-section was. I knew the clinical description. I knew the risks.

But nothing prepared me for seeing my wife laid out like that, the great bloody spreading wound, her bladder outside of her body, resting on her belly. There were hands moving within her, flesh being tugged, blood ...

I almost fell over. And I have never loved her as deeply as I did at that moment. She is the strongest person I have ever met.

And I couldn't even cut the cord.

I think I was escorted out of the operating room. I don't remember taking off my scrubs.

A nurse brought Xander out. He was swaddled up tight, and silent. And he was wearing a hat. When the nurse removed it, I could see that his head, covered in brown hair, tapered to a rounded point, like an old intercontinental missile. "That's from pushing against the pelvic brim," she said, replacing the cap. "There was no way he was coming out on his own."

And then I was alone with him, for the first time. My son. Suddenly burst forth from imagination and conjecture into the world. I snugged him close. I whispered his name into his ear.

There's a photo taken that day or the next. In it, I'm holding Xander slightly away from myself, both of his feet on my chest. I'm leaning slightly forward, enraptured, and he's looking back, tiny and pale.

You can almost see our eyes meet.

The way the light falls on his face, the way it seems to shine back at me. It feels holy. Sacred.

It feels like living proof.

Well now on a summer night in a dusky room
Come a little piece of the Lord's undying light
Crying like he swallowed the fiery moon
In his mother's arms it was all the beauty I could take
Like the missing words to some prayer that I could never make
In a world so hard and dirty so fouled and confused
Searching for a little bit of God's mercy
I found living proof

Brilliant Disguise

Album: *Tunnel of Love*
Released: October 9, 1987
Recorded: January–July 1987
Version discussed: VH1 *Storytellers*, recorded April 4, 2005
Album/released: VH1 *Storytellers* DVD, released September 6, 2005

O
N APRIL 4, 2005, Bruce Springsteen took the stage of the Two River Theater in Red Bank, New Jersey, for a performance unlike any other he had ever given. As part of VH1's *Storytellers* series, he appeared on a bare stage with only his songbook, a harmonica, a piano, and a guitar.[1] Springsteen had, of course, performed solo and acoustic previously—for the entire *Ghost of Tom Joad* tour, for example, which took him around the world over a period of eighteen months. He had also done an audience question-and-answer period before, at the two concerts he performed in support of *Double Take* magazine in Somerville, Massachusetts, in early 2003.

---

1. Actually, a series of guitars. This is one thing I don't get about Springsteen. I've watched Richard Thompson—arguably one of the finest guitar players on the planet—perform a two-hour solo acoustic show using one guitar for the whole thing. So why is it necessary for Springsteen to change guitars for every song? I know about different tunings, different tones, all of that, but it seems excessive. And irksome. On a tangential guitar note: there's a moment in most shows with the band when, standing at the front of the stage, he'll take his guitar off and throw it back towards the drum kit—without turning or looking. It's caught, every time, by his guitar tech. The move is spectacular, and always gets a cheer, but you have to wonder: how shitty would it feel to not make that catch some night?

But the *Storytellers* performance was different by design—it wasn't just a concert, it was an inquiry into process, inspiration, and creation. As the title suggests, it was to be an evening's worth of stories. And Springsteen delivered. Over the course of almost two hours, he dissected eight songs spanning his career, discussing his songwriting process, exploring references and connections, and laying bare both his craft and his soul.

As he takes the stage, Springsteen is clearly uncomfortable,[2] and the opening discussion of "Devils & Dust,"[3] while interesting, is stilted and clearly scripted. His comments about "Blinded by the Light," while revelatory and frequently hilarious, are also stagey and deliberate.

He seems to find his groove as the show progresses, however, along with a level of comfort that allows him to make some stunning disclosures. Most significant among these, for me, is what he says about his public face and his private self and how they interact. "I didn't write very well about men and women until 1987," he confides during his introduction to "Brilliant Disguise." "I wasn't doin' it very well either. Maybe that had something to do with it."

The song, which was the lead-off single from *Tunnel of Love* has always been about the impenetrability and falseness of the faces we show the world, and the impossibility of true intimacy, even with ourselves. On the *Storytellers* stage, it becomes a vessel for honesty and disclosure.[4] "We all have multiple selves," Springsteen says. "That's just the way we're built. We've got sort of this public self, this public face we show to others. I'm wearing mine right now."

---

2. He cops to the strangeness of the idea of discussing his creative process by describing it as "an iffy proposition." He continues by saying, "Talking about music is like talking about sex. Can you describe it? Are you supposed to?"

3. The appearance on *Storytellers* was ostensibly to promote the 2005 *Devils & Dust* album.

4. This raises a question, of course: how much of this candidness about his two faces was, in fact, candor, and how much of it was artifice and construct? The same can be asked, of course, about any sort of disclosive art, from confessional poetry to self-portraits to memoirs written in the guise of liner notes.

Springsteen goes on to recount his fondness for strip clubs and mentions two people who have objected to his going: his wife and "that holier-than-thou bastard Bruce Springsteen." He describes meeting fans as he was leaving a strip club, one of whom remarked "Bruce, you're not supposed to be here." His response—that he's a figment of Springsteen that "Bruce does not even know [is] missing"—is surreal, with the ring of truth.

Springsteen's revelations about his two selves are significant enough, considering the piety with which he is often regarded by his fans. But he continues, describing how "Brilliant Disguise" has changed for him, over time, from a song about the separation of identities to a hymn of communion. "When you sing the song with somebody you love it turns into something else, I think. It becomes a song of a reaffirmation of the world's mysteries, its shadows, our frailties and the acceptance of those frailties, without which there is no love."

The acceptance of those frailties.

Patti Scialfa joins him on stage for the version of the song that follows. It's beautiful and haunting, and it changes in exactly the way Springsteen said it would. There are still secrets, still questions, and there always will be. That's the nature of the world.

And the world, as the poet[5] says, is always too much with us, late and soon. Watching Springsteen and Scialfa on that stage, the love so thick between them it's almost a physical thing, it's easy to idealize their relationship. You don't have to dig too deeply, though, to understand that their happiness is hard won, a trial by fire. It's not just strip clubs. Rumors of Springsteen's lack of fidelity—and his stays in the "barn," an outbuilding[6] on their Runsom, N.J., property, often for weeks or months at a time—appear frequently in the mainstream media and are whispered among fans online.

---

5. William Wordsworth, for the record.
6. Which, let's face it, is probably far larger and nicer than any home most of us are ever likely to visit.

Longtime fans hold that his concerts are looser, his interactions with the crowd more liberal, when Patti is at home with the kids. He's playing for the ladies; he always has.[7]

Public faces, private lives. Public lies, and the truths we only tell in the night, when only one person is listening.

It's true for all of us.

IT'S ABOUT a four-hour drive from the Peace Arch border crossing to Portland, Oregon, on a good day. Add in the drive time from the ferry terminal, and the wait at the border, and you're looking at five plus.

It was late afternoon, August. High summer, and the heat felt like a wall coming.

It was less than two weeks into the 2002 tour for *The Rising*, and Greg and I were doing back-to-back shows, Portland and Tacoma. Springsteen Inc. was trying something new with this tour: a general admission floor, with a fenced-off area in front of the stage for the first three hundred or so fans in line.

We were determined to be in the pit, and that meant taking an extra day off work to get there in time.

The early part of the drive passed with the usual banalities: work, writing, reports from earlier shows on the tour, expectations from the setlist, plans for our day in the lineup.

We stopped for dinner, and when we came out, it was getting dark. Back in the car, we put on *Roses and Broken Hearts*, a bootleg from the *Tunnel of Love* tour.

It was going to be that kind of night. A Circle night.

Sometimes it's hard to tell how these things begin.[8]

---

7. There's a great moment in Peter Weir's film *Dead Poets Society* when Robin Williams, playing a renegade English teacher, asks a class of private school boys why men write poetry. He dismisses the usual pieties, before answering his own question: "To woo women." One can't deny the insight.

8. One of my favorite lines, from anywhere, comes early in the musical *The Fantasticks*: "You wonder how these things begin," the narrator, El Gallo, says of the two young lovers. To me, that's as magical as "Once upon a time," and more evocative.

Was it going out for pie at the Lakeview Diner in Harrison when I was home from university for weekends?

Or was it those afternoons on the beach, with our broken hearts and our woman-hating music?

Was it those dawn mornings, picking strawberries in neighboring rows?

Was it before even that, back in home ec, talking about jerking off and heavy metal?

Where did the Circle of Men begin?

Ultimately, I suppose it doesn't matter. What matters is that it still exists, this magic Circle.

It exists over pie or breakfast at three AM in roadside diners, throats raw following a show.

It exists in dive bars in strange cities, chain smoking and drinking crappy beer before passing out in a cheap hotel room.

And it exists on the highway in the middle of the night, lights from oncoming cars flashing through the windshield, Springsteen coming out of the stereo, voices hushed and no eye contact being made.

The Circle of Men is a term Greg thought of, and it comes with its own rules. Chief among them is that nothing leaves the Circle: what is talked about there stays there.[9]

(I'm adhering to that, by the way. Greg has read these pages, and anything you see here has been released willingly from the Circle. No confidences will have been violated, no lines crossed.)[10]

I've discovered over the years that I don't really *do* casual acquaintances. I don't have so-so friends. I recognize that this is an issue—I need more guy friends I can just hang out with, shoot the shit with over a couple of beers.[11]

---

9. It occurs to me that the Circle of Men is the sensitive-guy version of *Fight Club*, a non-hippie version of that mid-nineties *Iron John* crap.

10. Peter doesn't figure into this chapter, but he's also part of the Circle. For the two of us, it's usually parsing our lives over cigars in downtown Toronto, usually after a night of drinking, usually before I have to catch a plane.

11. This is where a tolerance for sports would come in handy: hanging out to watch the

That's not the way it works for me, though. I gravitate toward intense friendships. Greg and Peter and me? Nothing is off the table. No truth too hard, no secret too deep.

When you've sat beside a friend as his heart is breaking, as he cries, listening to "Point Blank," there's nothing casual about that. When you've split a pair of earphones so you can both listen to a bootleg of Springsteen singing "Can't Help Falling in Love," because you are both doing just that—in a sort of teenage doomed frenzy—there's nothing casual about that.

And when you spend four hours in a car at night, hurtling down a highway at seventy miles an hour, telling secrets? There's nothing casual about that.

It started off casually enough, though: we talked about the show we were listening to, and I gave Greg the expected hard time about not coming to Tacoma with Peter and me. He replied with the usual comment about the unused ticket from the 1992 tour.

When we got to "All That Heaven Will Allow," though, the conversation turned more personal.

On the *Tunnel of Love* tour, Springsteen ditched many of his standard numbers (no "Badlands," no "Thunder Road," no "The Promised Land"), and largely dispensed with the rambling, seemingly spontaneous song introductions that had characterized previous tours.

He did have a park bench, though.

"All That Heaven Will Allow" is a nakedly romantic song,[12] an ode to love and to the power of a good relationship to brighten even the worst day. On the tour, it was introduced every night by a

---

game is the perfect casual-guy-friend thing to do. Sadly? I still don't give a fuck about hockey, and apparently my derision comes through. There is, however, a men's book club that I've visited on occasion. I have a standing invitation to join; as soon as this book is done, I think I might do that.

12. With all of the darkness of *Tunnel of Love*, it's easy to overlook that there are some beautiful, romantic songs on the album as well. "All that Heaven Will Allow" and "Tougher Than the Rest" are two of the finest loves songs Springsteen has ever written.

bit of theatre. Springsteen and Clemons would take a seat on a park bench on stage and talk about, well, girls.

When the introduction came on that night in the car with Greg, our conversation turned, naturally enough, to our own "park bench" days: those summers at the beach.

"So what are your five biggest regrets?" he asked me at one point.

I thought for a moment. "I don't regret anything I've ever done," I said, staring out at the lights and the darkness. "The things I didn't do…"

"Jenn," he said, correctly, with the certainty reserved for old friends.

"What about you?"

He had a list.

When he was done, it was my turn to ask a question. "What are the best things you've done?"

He talked about going to grad school, moving out of Vancouver into the hinterland to get teaching experience. He talked about his daughters.

The night continued like that, swapping questions back and forth.

What's the worst thing you've ever done?

If you could do one thing over?

What was your worst moment?

We talked about everything. Nothing was off the table. We talked about the frustrations of the day to day, about what it was like being a father, what had surprised us and what hadn't. We talked about our sex lives, how things were different now that there were babies in the house, how things were after pregnancy and childbirth. We were completely candid, completely open.

Except… I wasn't.

It's strange. Greg knows more about me than just about anyone in the world, but I froze. He knows every dirty thing I've done, every shame, every failing, and he has never, not once, judged or scorned.

But I couldn't tell him how I was feeling.

I couldn't tell him how scared I was about being a father, how uncertain. Cori seemed to do everything so naturally, and the other new fathers we knew seemed to take to it so effortlessly. I stumbled at every turn. It wasn't just the practicalities, I had no idea how to *be*. How could I get out of my own head enough to really connect with the little boy who was looking to me? Could I really put myself aside in favor of someone else?

And it wasn't just fatherhood. I spent most of my days completely overwhelmed. There was always too much work, and never enough money. Never enough time, and always too much to do. I'd turned miserable and I was pretty much sad all the time.

But how could I say that to Greg? Just the thought of it made me feel so weak, so inferior. I felt like such a failure so much of the time—saying it out loud would only add to it.

So the questions continued.

A lot of the answers we knew each other well enough to anticipate; some of our questions were asked specifically to elicit those responses. And there were some surprises.

I hadn't realized, for example, how much Greg had suffered over his height, the amount of torment he had taken at school about being the big man. He had always seemed so impervious. It was something we had never talked about, and the realization crushed me.

There was something different about Greg that night, some chip in the veneer.

"Are you happy?" I asked, when it was my turn. I kept my eyes focused on the road ahead. Deliberately.

He answered slowly. He talked about his daughters again, and his job, and his prospects. He talked about coaching senior girls basketball, about giving something back. He talked about Agassiz, and the new house, and his plans for the yard.

He didn't really answer the question.

Greg started dating Lisa shortly after I started dating Cori. They got married about a year after we did.

I didn't need him to answer the question in the car that night; I had known the answer for years.[13]

I glanced over at him quickly. He was hunched down a bit, peering through the windshield, his hands tight around the wheel.

"So, Cori," he said. "If you met her today, would you marry her again?"

I thought of the sadness I was feeling, all the doubt, the deep certainty of my failure as a father and a man.

"Yes," I said.

I knew better than to ask the question in return.

"I think that's our exit," I said, pointing at the sign overhanging the highway. "Coming up on the right."

> So when you look at me
> you better look hard and look twice
> Is that me baby
> or just a brilliant disguise?

---

13. Greg got married for the second time in November 2010. He married Wendy, a lovely woman who he's worked with for years, and the affection and passion between them is pervasive and strong. She loves his daughters, and they love her. I was in Toronto on book tour, so I couldn't be there, but Peter and I had a couple of drinks in their honor over the course of the evening.

The Rising

Album: *The Rising*
Released: July 30, 2002
Recorded: January–March 2002

T HE LEGEND[1] goes like this:

The attacks on the World Trade Center, September 11, 2001, were very close to Bruce Springsteen, both geographically and emotionally. Monmouth County, where Springsteen and Scialfa live with their family on a farm near Colts Neck, is close enough to New York City to be home to many people employed in the financial industry in lower Manhattan. The Al Qaeda attacks were devastating to the community, many areas of which had clear views across to Manhattan, to the columns of smoke where the towers had once stood. Of the 341 firefighters who died that day, 158 were from Monmouth County.

Following the attacks, Springsteen did what he apparently does when troubled: he drove around. And as he was driving, the story goes, a car pulled up next to him at a light, and a window was unrolled. "Bruce," someone is said to have called, "We need you now."

Within weeks, Springsteen had the band back in the studio, and early the next summer his first album of new material in seven

---

1. I know, I know. You can't believe everything you hear. Ironically? It was Bruce Springsteen who taught me that, in his 1985 introduction to his cover of Edwin Starr's "War": "Blind faith in your leaders, or in anything, will get you killed." Blindly believing a rock star about his inspiration probably isn't as potentially lethal, but consider a grain of salt judiciously taken.

years, *The Rising*, hit record-store shelves on a wave of hype the likes of which Springsteen's career hadn't seen since the glory days of *Born in the U.S.A.*

It's a great story, but was the prototypical man of the people actually summoned by the people to resume his work, to heal them with his words?

We'll never know.

But we do know, since it's been reported and verified, that in the wake of the 9/11 attacks, Springsteen spent a lot of time reading the obituaries of those who had died, especially those in the rescue services. In those first painful weeks after the attacks, an odd thing would sometimes happen. A grieving widow would be at home, and the phone would ring, and a familiar voice would say, "This is Bruce Springsteen," offering words of comfort for their loss. A number of the reported calls lasted more than an hour. Springsteen also provided new versions of several of his songs, recorded for individual heroes, to be played at their funerals.

He did what he could to help soothe the pain of his community in those horrifying first weeks.[2]

And in the months after that, he wrote furiously. He brought the band back together for their first studio album in eighteen years,[3] and over a period of less than a month they recorded at least fifteen new songs.

---

2. Look, I'm sitting here with tears streaming down my face, and I'm not sure that I know why. I think it's this, though: the man is in the upper ranks of rock royalty. He's richer than Croesus, and his every public appearance is an event. So here he is, in the aftermath of a national tragedy, and what's he doing? He's calling people who have lost someone. He's talking to them, asking about the people they've lost, listening to their stories. He's giving the gift of his music in their memory. He's giving his time. He's giving of himself. There's a lot to be cynical about with Springsteen, especially considering the amount of hype that accompanied the release of *The Rising* months later, but credit where credit is due: he did more than you or I did, or would have been tempted to do. And it made a difference. Holy fuck. Yeah, I'm verklempt. Talk amongst yourselves.

3. It's strange to think that *Born in the U.S.A.* was the last Springsteen album to feature The E Street Band, but 'tis true: *Tunnel of Love* was essentially a Springsteen solo album, and after that the band was very publically shit-canned.

The Rising was unlike anything he and the band had ever done. Part of that was by design. Springsteen had broken up the band after the *Tunnel of Love* tour because, among other reasons, he wanted to pursue different sounds. The band's triumphant reunion tour of 1999–2000, while it was many, many impressive things, in other ways served to codify the band's strengths as excesses. To remedy this, Springsteen now changed his approach. For the first time in decades, the band worked with an outside producer, Brendan O'Brien, who had previously worked with Pearl Jam and Rage Against the Machine. They recorded on the fly, at O'Brien's Atlanta studio, rather than taking up residency at one of their traditional haunts. Springsteen brought in violinist Soozie Tyrell to freshen the sound. He experimented with different musical styles, including the Sufi inflections of "Worlds Apart," which featured qaawali musician Asif Ali Khan and his group.

More striking than the sonic differences were some of the approaches Springsteen took to the songs. Although a number of the pieces pre-date September 11, 2001, the songs written after the attacks reflect not only an immersion in the events, but also a deeply personal understanding of their effect on the people around him.

It is impossible to hear songs like "You're Missing" (which details a day of loss, from a morning normal in every way save the absence of a partner, to the children in the evening asking if their parent will be coming home) or the rollicking "Mary's Place" (which details a house party so suffused in loss that one assumes it's a wake) and not think of the survivors with whom Springsteen spent so much time. He's once again chronicling his community, but this time with a personal connection; these aren't the existential figures that populated *Darkness on the Edge of Town*. Yet he also pushes beyond that personal experience. You might expect "Into the Fire," an uplifting near-hymn about being inspired by heroism, from Springsteen, but few people were prepared for either "Paradise," which sympathetically follows a young suicide bomber, or

"Empty Sky," which deals with both the desire for vengeance and the futility of acting upon that desire.

And then there was "The Rising" itself.

In many ways, the album's title track is the most typical "Springsteen song" on the record.[4] It's got a rousing sing-along chorus, it's got great show-opening power, it's bigger than life.

It's also transcendent. As should be the case for an album's title song, it's here that many of the record's themes and concerns coalesce. "The Rising" is the song most explicitly about 9/11, following a rescue worker to the scene of a disaster and up a smoke-filled staircase, but it never succumbs to the details. Instead of tragedy, it's a song of ascension, a glorious moment of... well, rising. With its bells, its cross, and its "wheels of fire," with its Mary and its dream of life, it is the most explicitly spiritual song Springsteen has ever written, in the guise of one of his most topical.

On the ensuing tour, opening with "The Rising," a song about the vitality of a "dream of life," and closing every night with "Land of Hope and Dreams," a gospel-tinged train song about inclusiveness and a golden promised land into which all will be welcomed, Springsteen seemed to be deliberately creating, every night, a celebration of life, not only its bright spots but also its darkness, and its questions.

Take five minutes and watch "The Rising" on the *Live in Barcelona* DVD. Watch the reactions of the audience, the hand claps as the song begins, the arms in the air, the synchronicity, the responsiveness to Springsteen's every gesture, his every word—everyone in the building is part of the song. This isn't an audience, it's a congregation, and the message of the show is clear: life is complicated and hard, and at the same time something holy and profound. It's a journey, over three hours, through the light and the dark.

---

4. I know, I'm ignoring "Waitin' on a Sunny Day," which is the sort of cheer-inducing pop ditty that the man can write in his sleep. And may have. I file this one with "Hungry Heart": yes, I know people like it. I'm not one of those people.

GREG AND I arrived in Portland around three in the morning. By that point, I think we were navigating mostly on faith, but we drove directly off the interstate and up to one of the main entrances of the Rose Garden Arena.[5] Parking the car in a loading zone, we started to wander, with only a vague idea of what we were looking for.

It took no more than a couple of minutes to find it: near the entrance there was a post with a clipboard attached, and a list had been started. Greg and I used the pen affixed to the clipboard with a length of string and wrote our names beside numbers seven and eight.

On the way back to the car, we high-fived each other.[6] We had done it—we were going to be in the pit.

Ah, the pit.

When tickets for the *Rising* tour first went on sale, the Springsteen organization announced that they were doing away with the "jailbait"[7] system from the reunion tour and going over to general admission on the floor. General admission with a twist, as I mentioned in the last chapter. Right in front of the stage for every show would be a fenced-off area reserved for the first three hundred or so fans through the door.[8]

In the absence of any pit policies or procedures from the organization, the fans took over. Lineups were strictly monitored, with

---

5. I've tried to navigate that area of Portland in a non-exhausted state and encountered frustration after frustration. That we got to the arena so easily is mind-boggling.

6. Technically, I suppose Greg low-fived my high-five. So what's that, a median-five?

7. "Jailbait" is the term fans used to describe the policy of having the first seventeen rows of seating on the floor available only by phone, with tickets being picked up in person on the day of the show with proper ID. This was to—theoretically—prevent the scalping of the best tickets in the house, to make sure the fans had equal access. The nickname? First seventeen rows: under eighteen. Jailbait.

8. Response to the pit divided fans. Some saw the merit in rewarding the most devoted fans, those willing to spend all day in line to get closest to the stage. Others saw it as unfair, and punitive to those fans who couldn't take a full day off work to get that close. I was—and am—firmly in the fair reward camp. As someone who had to travel hundreds of miles and miss a few days of work to see a couple of shows, I liked the idea of my diligence being rewarded.

people signing in when they arrived, their number in line noted on a master list and marked on their hand in felt pen. You had to be in line for regular check-ins, but in between you could get away to find food or a bathroom without losing your spot. It was, to my mind, an equitable system.[9]

Greg and I had been planning to spend the night in the car, but he suggested we try the hotel we had reserved for after the show instead. (We had seats for the next show in Tacoma; the plan was to sleep in, drive leisurely up to the Tacoma Dome, and to arrive just before showtime. A chill day.) In one of the earliest check-ins in recorded history, we got our room just before four AM, and slept for a couple of hours before heading back to the arena. When we arrived, shortly after six, there was already a crowd.

We spent the day on the concrete outside the arena. It was hot, and there was no shade, but we didn't care. Greg went off to procure breakfast, and we took occasional walks between check-ins, but most of the time we just hung out. We met fans from all over Canada and the U.S. People we knew from the newsgroup and people we knew by reputation. We met tapers,[10] and a guy writing a book about Springsteen who was following the tour from stop to stop. A large contingent had already been to a few shows on the tour (which had only started two weeks before), including the one two days previous in Las Vegas, so we listened to their carefully hedged stories. (They were dying to brag and enthuse, but they didn't want to spoil the show for newbies like us).

It wasn't all hearts and flowers. A vocal, simmering group splintered off and started a second line at one of the other doors. Fans

---

9. Of course, any system is open to corruption, and as the tour progressed, stories began to pile up about multiple lists, multiple wristbands, fake numbers, and "pit pigs," fans who were front and center night after night. *Sic transit Gloria.*

10. In the days before everyone could record and film shows with their cell phones, tapers—the folks who would invest in quality equipment to record shows in the best possible sound—got a lot more respect. When it comes to bootlegs, I much prefer to wait for higher quality than to succumb to the siren call of instant gratification.

arriving throughout the day were frustrated both by the lineup and the limited opportunity to butt into it. Things never descended into an outright clusterfuck (a favored term of my online friend Caryn, whom I met for the first time that day), but they came close a couple of times.

And the run through the arena—after an agonizing wait for the wristbands that would allow us back into the pit should we need to fetch beers, say, or use the restroom—racing the people from the second entrance? That's something I'd rather forget.

But leaning against the lip of the stage just past Patti's microphone, none of that mattered. We'd done it. Hundreds of miles. No sleep. A full day in line. Front fucking row.

That was the moment Greg and I started what would become the tradition of calling Peter on one of our cell phones. Without saying hello, we held the phone next to the stage as we pounded it. "Front row, baby," Greg crowed, before hanging up.[11]

We spent close to two hours more standing up, waiting. Springsteen is famous for starting shows late. You might think we would have been annoyed, but nothing was harshing our buzz (including the women behind us irritated by Greg's height).

And when the lights went down...

I thought I knew everything I needed to know about Springsteen. I could have told you his biography in chapter and verse. I had seen shows. I could talk bootlegs and alternate takes, setlists from past tours and other arcana. I knew, from bootlegs, exactly the count-off that would herald a particular song. I was steeped. I was informed. I had been a fan for almost twenty years. I knew my shit.

---

11. This is, of course, a bit of an asshole thing to do. I know that. I recognized it in the moment, even as I was pounding on the stage. I recognize the assholeness every time I do it. And I do it anyway. Peter would expect nothing less of us. (The only time we didn't do it was during the *Magic* tour, when he booked time off and bought flights and tickets to join us for a three-show swing, only to get snowed under with work and have to cancel at the last moment. To call him under those circumstances—despite standing right in front of Clarence in Vancouver—would have been cruel.)

Until the moment the band entered, though, in pairs, up a stairway at the back of a stage, Bruce[12] and Clarence bringing up the rear... until the moment that Bruce counted into the first song... until the moment that the mighty mighty E Street Band came to life with the force of a hurricane...

It was only with "The Rising" that I got it, that I understood, deep in my soul, what it all meant to me. I went to a place beyond words, a place of surrender and exultation, a place where everything made sense.

I spent the next three hours transported. I abandoned myself to songs like "Prove It All Night" and "Backstreets." I thought of Peter when Bruce did "Bobby Jean" and again during "Born to Run," electric and full band this time, Bruce playing the arena of fans as much as he was playing his guitar.

In only the second week of the tour, with a full album of new material, it was fascinating to watch Springsteen actively conducting the band, gesturing for changes, occasionally disappointed. Everything that would within a few months seem like second nature was in its early stages.

Numerous times over the course of the night Springsteen worked the crowd from right in front of us, close enough to touch. The crowd surged forward at these moments, hands flailing, desperate for the slightest contact. They crushed me against the stage. But I wasn't part of that flailing. I'm not afflicted by that sort of hero worship. I didn't want to touch the hem of Springsteen's garment or the guitar; I wanted the chance to watch him play from inches away. And I got it.[13]

There were a lot of songs it thrilled me to hear. He introduced "Atlantic City," one of my favorites, by mentioning that he had

---

12. As I reread this, I noticed something interesting. Throughout this book, Springsteen has been Springsteen, subject and object, held at a distance. As soon as I lost myself in the memory of that show, though, he became Bruce. This is how fans talk, with an intimacy that belies the divide between performer and audience.

13. Cori's first question, upon hearing my description of the concert, was, "Did you get sweated on?" Yes. Yes I believe I was sweated on.

gotten married in Portland, not far from the arena. "Thunder Road" was incredible. And "Born to Run"? It may just be the perfect rock song, a roaring engine of escape and consequences.

But to my surprise, the songs I connected with most intensely were all new, or relatively so: "The Rising," "Into the Fire," and "Land of Hope and Dreams."

It's difficult to explain. All three songs took me out of myself while immersing me in myself. During "The Rising" I was one of a sea of individuals participating in the call and response, arms in the air in what seemed almost part of a choreographed dance. It felt like church, but not like the United Church services of my childhood. I could feel this in my soul.

"Into the Fire," with its narrative of heroism and sacrifice, was a potent reminder that there was a place for true nobility, true courage, in the world. All that stuff I was carrying, all that stuff I couldn't tell Greg in the car, seemed to pale before the reality of life and death.

"Land of Hope and Dreams" brought it home. A train song, based seemingly in equal parts on Woody Guthrie's "This Train Is Bound for Glory" and Curtis Mayfield's "People Get Ready," it's a valediction, a journey to the golden valley that awaits all who get on board. And anyone who wants to climb aboard can: the train carries everyone, from whores and gamblers to the broken-hearted.

A Springsteen show can change you. When I say, "You really have to see him live," I'm not resorting to cliché: those are words of experience.

Leaving the show that night, Greg and I were spent. It had been a long, long day, and we wanted nothing more than to sleep. We went back to the hotel and collapsed.

When I woke up the next morning, Greg was already awake.

"So, I was thinking," he said.

"Yeah." I already knew where this was going. I was already in motion.

We raced up to the Tacoma Dome and got a place in the general admission line. We managed to score a couple of scalper's tickets for the floor and sold one of our seats. We were meeting friends there, but we figured they would understand.[14] We spent another day under the hot sun, eating one of the world's biggest sandwiches for breakfast, lunch, and dinner combined. We raced with hundreds of other fans down a terrifying concrete stairwell and across the arena floor. We ended up almost exactly where we had been the night before, stage left, just in front of Patti.

How could we not? Having experienced that once, how could we pass up the chance to experience it again?

We called Peter. We pounded the stage.

We waited.

A dream of life comes to me
Like a catfish dancin' on the end of the line

---

14. Greg filled me in on a blank from that night as he was reading this manuscript: "During the Tacoma show, John was sitting forty rows up on the side of the stage in the upper deck, worried that we hadn't arrived. The houselights came on during 'Born to Run' and he turned to his friend and said, 'They're in the front row!'"

Dancing in the Dark

Album: *Born in the U.S.A.*
Released: June 4, 1984
Recorded: January 1982–March 1984

TRY THOUGH I might, there's no way I can reinvent history. So it's like this, and always will be: Bruce Springsteen became a superstar not because of his best albums (like *Darkness on the Edge of Town* or *Nebraska*) or his finest songs (like "Racing in the Street" or "Incident on 57th Street"), but because of a hook-laden, synth-based, dance-friendly single written with the sole intention of producing a hit.

Late in the sessions for *Born in the U.S.A.*, Springsteen was harangued by manager and producer Jon Landau, who, upon examining the album's projected running order, discerned the absence of a breakout single. Springsteen initially resisted, but within a couple of days had delivered the final track, the song that would make him a household name around the world.

The success of "Dancing in the Dark" was fostered not only by its radio-friendliness, but also by the winning rock video directed by Brian De Palma and the seven- and twelve-inch dance remixes that earned the song heavy rotation in clubs over the summer of 1984.

As Springsteen's popularity picked up steam, new singles followed, including "Born in the U.S.A.," "Glory Days," "I'm On Fire," and "My Hometown." Eventually, seven of the album's twelve songs were released as singles, all of them reaching the Billboard Top Ten.[1] "Dancing in the Dark" was the big one, though.

It's the song that changed everything.

It's the Springsteen song that everyone knows.

Despite this, it's pretty clear to me that not many people have actually listened to the words.

"Dancing in the Dark" is one of the poppiest, most radio-friendly, danceable and saccharine-sounding tracks you'll ever hear. But lyrically, it's one of the bleakest, most unrelenting songs in the Springsteen catalogue. The characters he created for the *Darkness on the Edge of Town* album—hell, even the narrator of "Point Blank"— have nothing on the sheer, existential dread that is "Dancing in the Dark."[2]

Take out the liner notes—or visit brucespringsteen.net—and read the lyrics. Now, read them again.

Stripped of its poppy veneer, "Dancing in the Dark" is the sound of a soul in torment, a man dragging himself through life without passion, lacking any "spark" to "start a fire" that's long gone out. If it ever existed.

He lives in a dump, and he's getting nowhere; he wants to change everything about himself, but he's utterly helpless. As the song progresses, the tension mounts. He's looking for love, but more than that, he's looking for even a single person to glance his way, to assure him that he still actually exists. And there's no respite,

---

1. Interestingly, none of the singles hit number one on the Billboard chart. "Dancing in the Dark" was blocked first by Duran Duran's "The Reflex," then by Prince's "When Doves Cry." Yes, I appreciate the irony of Springsteen's synth-pop gambit being chart-blocked by the pretty-boy synth kings in Duran Duran. And, hey, "When Doves Cry" is just a fantastic song.

2. As I was writing this, I posted this observation on Facebook and Twitter—never have I posted anything that has started so much dialogue, or caused so much disagreement. Several people argued that "The River" was Springsteen's most existentially wrought song. Some argued "The Promise." "State Trooper" and "Stolen Car" were both mentioned. These are all valid contenders, but I stand by my point. And fuck, it's my book, so...

no last-verse cry of defiance, just his growing desperation as he becomes more and more numb to everything in the world.

Springsteen has attempted, to little effect, to reclaim some of the inherent darkness of "Dancing in the Dark" over the last two decades. An acoustic version performed occasionally on the 1992–93 tour highlighted the words, but it didn't really work as a song. The hard-rocking, guitar-driven version of recent tours is a welcome relief from the twee synthesizers, but the musical treatment lends the song an air of defiance unsupported by the words.

The song is harrowing, and hearing it done this way casts a new light on the album as a whole. Born in the U.S.A., for all its chart-topping, trend-setting popularity, is almost uniformly bleak, from the traumatized veteran in the title song to the spurned lover in "I'm Goin' Down," from the aching loss of "Bobby Jean" to the desperate search for a lover not for passion but for protection in "Cover Me," from the good-times-turned-bad of "Darlington County" and "Working on the Highway," to the passionate, nay, psychotic desire of "I'm On Fire."

"Dancing in the Dark" reaches in to the listener, direct and unadorned. Springsteen's use of the first person in the verses establishes an intimacy, while the almost accusatory "you" in the chorus lends the song an air of complicity: I'm like this, and you know you're like this, too.

It's powerful stuff, and it's easy to imagine where it came from. Frustrated and tired at the end of a writing and recording process that spanned years,[3] Springsteen seems to have funneled

---

3. Yes, years. The songs that made up Nebraska, released in 1982, were, in many ways, the first demos of the Born in the U.S.A. sessions—those tracks date from early January of 1982, a home-recording session that also included early versions of "Born in the U.S.A.," "I'm Goin' Down," and "I'm On Fire." It was only when the sessions with the band in early 1982 failed to transform the bulk of those demos into E Street Band songs that it was decided to release them in their original form. Which, given the bleak, gut-wrenching nature of Nebraska, should have really served as a hint of just how dark Born in the U.S.A. was, despite the cheery flag cover and synthesizers.

his despair and exhaustion into a song he resolutely did not want to write. It's somewhat hard to imagine Springsteen as being this tortured—but perhaps the glossy trappings of the music are his way of attempting to hide it. In many ways, "Dancing in the Dark" is the song that most closely presages *Tunnel of Love*, his work in therapy, and the *Human Touch/Lucky Town* double-punch.

LURKING IN the shadows of Bruce Springsteen's songs and on-stage monologues, only occasionally making an appearance, is a gypsy woman, a fortune teller. She's the woman who promises a happy ending to the soon-to-be-married couple in "Brilliant Disguise," though it begins to seem, not too long after the wedding, that she was wrong, or that she lied. More promisingly, it is she who tells the singer, in the monologue during "Tenth Avenue Freeze-Out" on the reunion tour, that he needs a band (cue huge round of applause and band introductions).

It's easy to surmise that this figure is based, at least in part, on Madam Marie, the fortune teller on the Asbury Park boardwalk who is arrested in "4th of July, Asbury Park (Sandy)," though the fictional presence serves just as compellingly as a counterpoint to the Catholicism that runs rife through Springsteen's work.

There was a gypsy in my life, too.

Well, not so much a gypsy as a French teacher.

My French teacher in high school and I bonded early. She was nearly as unpopular with the administration as I was.

My notoriety resulted from a couple of... trends, shall we say... in my behavior. First, I had limited patience with what I felt—in retrospect, perhaps a little too self-righteously—were bullshit rules and regulations. I was always polite about it, but if something rubbed me the wrong way, I made my displeasure known, or simply ignored the rule altogether. Thus, not feeling I was getting anything out of my English 12 class, I would leave. I spent most of the year's worth of classes drinking coffee at Pang's Chinese restaurant. Second, I was unflinching in what I wrote, despite how it might be received, or what rules it might violate. Thus it was, for example, that I was almost expelled for a short film I wrote and directed that featured a student committing suicide.[4] Third, I was up front about what the administration seemed to consider bad behavior; it was common knowledge that my girlfriend and I were sleeping together, for example, a fact that didn't sit well with the devout principal (who happened to be the father of one of my closest friends).

My transgressions were clear; however, I was never sure what my French teacher had done wrong.

I do know she swore me to secrecy the day she read my tarot cards, warning me she would lose her job if anyone found out.

As if I would tell.

It was a quick reading, between classes one day. Three cards, focused on one question: would I become a writer?

It was the most important question I could ask. It was the only question that mattered.

As a kid, I was always scrawling in notebooks, taking inspiration from whatever I was watching or reading, ruthlessly plundering popular culture for inspiration. When I was obsessed with the *Alfred Hitchcock and the Three Investigators* series, I wrote mysteries with boy detectives. When I fell into the thrall of James Bond, first the movies, then the original Ian Fleming novels, I wrote spy pastiches, loaded with sex and imaginative—though highly derivative—violence.[5]

When the bullying was at its worst, I had my writing to retreat into, a world that was utterly my own. I wrote about the revenge I wanted to take, the violence I wanted to do in return for the violence done to me. I wrote about the mass murder of my tormentors,

---

4. I have never felt closer to my mother than I did the day she, upon being invited to visit the principal's office to discuss the issue, proceeded to lacerate the principal on my behalf. She's the reason I wasn't expelled, and why the film went on to represent the school in a province-wide competition.

5. When I was in grade seven, I asked one of the English teachers to read one of my spy novels—thirty or forty pages of badly printed looseleaf in a Duo-Tang. He was generous and careful in his response, especially when I asked him what he thought of the sex scenes. "Well," he said, measuredly. "There's a reason you don't buy shoes from a snake."

about torching the school, and about being "saved" by the girl who I had an incredible crush on.

When I was falling in love, I wrote love stories. When my heart was broken, I wrote sad stories.[6] When I was close to graduating, I wrote stories about kids leaving home or living out their last summers in their small hometowns.[7]

I'd chosen UVic because it had the best creative writing program in the province at that time.[8] I had no vision of any future except that of being a writer. I didn't have the faintest idea what that might actually be like, except that there would probably be girls and I'd finally be popular. But I had to know. I had to know whether it was just a silly dream. I needed someone to tell me that I was on the right track.

So I asked the gypsy.

My French teacher looked at the cards carefully, then looked at me.

"According to the cards," she said, "you're going to write a lot. A lot of short things. And it looks like there's a chance you'll be very popular very fast."

I could feel my blood starting to rise.

"But," she said, and I cooled, "if you don't have that early success, you're going to have to wait a long time. Ten years? Maybe more?"

She tucked the cards away, and we never spoke of it again.

Was she just being kind, and telling me what I wanted to hear while tempering it with caution? Was she just not very good at the whole tarot thing?

---

6. Of course, it is not that easy. One of my mother's recurring questions in those years was, "Why can't you write anything happy?" I suspect she still asks herself that, but she's given up on asking me.

7. Over the Labor Day weekend in 1987, I entered the 3-Day Novel Contest, a marathon session that requires you to write a novel in, well, three days. The book I ended up with was a fractured collection of vignettes about couples making love in deserted boathouses, friends getting high and throwing rocks off of overpasses, parties down by the river's edge, and young lovers saying goodbye, all set on the Sunday of the Labor Day weekend. I called it *Soft Summer*, drawn from the first line in Bruce Springsteen's "Backstreets."

8. Well, that was the stated reason. We all know the truth by now, don't we?

Or was it, in fact, my fortune? That I'd either make it right out of the gate or spend a long time trying?

I went to UVic and joined the creative writing program. I wrote stories and short plays, submitted things to magazines. I read voraciously, and I wrote for *The Martlet*, the student newspaper. Cori and I were seeing each other by that point, and she would take photos for my newspaper stories, and edit my fiction.

That instant success? It seemed to be a while in coming.

I transferred out of the creative writing program and into English. I wrote, a lot, keeping Cori busy with her red pen. I got a job in a bookstore. I read like a fiend. I submitted my stories around.

Still no instant success.

And somewhere inside me, a clock was ticking.

I graduated, and got caught up in the day to day, in work, in being married. The writing slowed down, then all but stopped.

The complacency of comfort.

I missed my window. I turned twenty-five, then twenty-six. Too old to be a wunderkind.

And then I got fired.

I could be colloquial and coy and say "I lost my job," the one that I missed my convocation for, the one I chose over my honeymoon. But no, this is no time for coyness: I got egregiously shit-canned, there one minute, gone the next.

The following morning, I got out of bed and started writing a short story, the first story I had started in years. It was a story about pregnancy and childbirth, a mythic tale focusing on the male journey through what is usually seen as exclusively a women's experience.

After I finished that, I wrote a novel.

And then another short story.

And another.

And then Cori got pregnant. I responded to the news by going a little insane and channeling all of my fears, all of my worst-case scenarios, into a manuscript about a little girl who gets hit by a truck.

Before I Wake was written in a white heat of fear over the first three months of 1999. I wrote it longhand, in the study of our new house, smoking cigarillos with the side door open in the middle of winter as I scrawled into my notebooks.

Once it was written, I left it. The notebooks sat undisturbed for a couple of years. There was no rush to go through the agony of transcribing it onto the computer: no one was waiting for it, and it was such a bizarre story it's not like anyone would be interested in publishing it anyway.

Eventually, though, I buckled down and did the typing. And when it was done, I was strangely pleased by what I had. It wasn't perfect, but I knew that with a little work it would be better. It might even be good.

So Cori and I worked it. Over and over, draft by draft, we made those notebooks into a novel.

We polished, and we honed, and when I thought it was ready, I sent the first section to an editor I had come to know over my past few trips to Toronto. That was March 2003.

The next month, I took the ferry over to Vancouver for the first show of the Canadian leg of the tour for *The Rising*. Greg and John picked me up, and we headed out to the old Pacific Coliseum. It was only eleven at night by the time we got there, but there were already more than fifty people in line.

It was, as Caryn would say,[9] a clusterfuck. The word was out about the pit, and everyone wanted to be in.

We got our names on the list, got our numbers, and crashed at Greg's in-laws' place for the night.

I don't know if I told Greg and John that I had sent the book out. I probably did. It was probably casual, like a *fait accompli*. I generally tried not to make too big of a deal out of anything to do with my writing. I couldn't let anyone see how important it was to me. How central to my being.

My mother, I'm sure, would have called it putting all of my eggs

---

9. She did say it, in fact: we met up with her the next day, and "clusterfuck" was one of the first words out of her mouth.

into one basket. Yet it was more than that, even. I had staked my whole life on one roll of the dice. One reader.

I had no idea what I would do if she didn't like it.

The show the next night was the show in which Springsteen allegedly audibled in "My Hometown" instead of "Incident on 57th Street." It was the show where John and I got mildly hammered when we discovered—after buying the beers—that they weren't allowed on the floor. What option did we have but to pound through the eight beers in less than twenty minutes? It was the show where we stood in front of Clarence for the first time, and I got to sing along at the top of my lungs to the final lines of "This Hard Land."

And it was the night I discovered I loved "Dancing in the Dark."

It was the guitar heavy version that we had first seen in Tacoma the year before, but now it seemed different. When he hit the line "I'm sick of sittin' round here trying to write this book," I laughed out loud. It was what I had been doing for months. It was exactly how I had been feeling.

That song's been a touchstone for me ever since. In 2008, at three shows in a row, I suspect my laughter might have been a little maniacal: I was mired in the depths of what would become *Bedtime Story*, my second published novel, which was then just a stack of notebooks with no end in sight.

But that moment in 2003, that first laugh of recognition? My manuscript was away, being looked at by an editor, and I knew that no matter what happened, whether it got published or went back into the drawer, I was a writer. It was like the gypsy woman had promised. I was right on schedule.

I'm dying for some action
I'm sick of sitting 'round here trying to write this book
I need a love reaction
come on now baby gimme just one look

Jesus Was an Only Son

Album: *Devils & Dust*
Released: April 26, 2005
Recorded: 1996–2004
Version discussed: VH1 *Storytellers*, recorded April 4, 2005
Album/released: VH1 *Storytellers* DVD, released September 6, 2005

DESPITE HIS POSITION atop the rock-and-roll pyramid, Springsteen has spent significant chunks of his career on the other, folkier side of the tracks.

As he recounts in his introduction to "Long Time Comin'" on the bonus DVD that accompanied the initial release of his *Devils & Dust* album: "I was signed as a guy with an acoustic guitar when I was twenty-two... I always, even when I was in my late teens, had a band, and then on another night I would go down to the coffee shop with my twelve-string and I would sing a whole group of songs that wouldn't work in a bar, or needed more attention, or were just... different."

With *Born to Run*, *Darkness on the Edge of Town*, and *The River*, Springsteen largely embraced his rock side, distancing himself from the folk elements present in *Greetings from Asbury Park, N.J.* (on "The Angel" in particular), and in *The Wild, the Innocent & the E Street Shuffle*. The folkie oompah of "Wild Billy's Circus Story" on the latter album is a jarring contrast to the rock-jazz elements of the other songs, but tunes like "Incident on 57th Street" and "New York City Serenade" reveal a singer-songwriter's eye for story.

Nebraska, the 1982 album which followed up the blockbuster success of *The River*, was something completely different. The stark, mournful, at times nihilistic collection was actually recorded by Springsteen at his New Jersey home in early 1982 using only an acoustic guitar, a harmonica, and a primitive mixing board hooked up to a cassette deck. The songs were demos, rough versions intended for the band, and they weren't considered for public release until the recording sessions failed to exceed their raw power.

Although widely regarded as *Nebraska's* folkie successor, *The Ghost of Tom Joad*, released in 1995, was intended for public consumption from the outset. For that reason, possibly, it lacks the naked intimacy of *Nebraska*, and feels overly self-conscious. It's also not a solo acoustic album; many of the tracks feature what you might call a folk-rock version of The E Street Band.[1]

The Ghost of Tom Joad is a solid album, and the title track has become a Springsteen classic,[2] but to me it feels like a case of too much reportage, not enough insight. Springsteen had done a lot of reading about life in the border country, the difficult lives of illegal immigrants, their role in the drug culture, their fate, and he channeled his research into his lyrics, creating complex stories that, in the main, failed to connect.

Ten years later, Springsteen released his third "folk" album, *Devils & Dust*. Another small-ensemble album—this time with a string section as well as a folk group comprising mainly E Street mainstays—the album met with limited success before virtually disappearing. That's not really surprising: the album was all over the map stylistically, cobbled together from songs as much as fifteen years old.[3] It also lacked solid thematic unity. "Devils & Dust"

---

1. Danny Federici on accordion and keyboards, Garry Tallent on bass, Soozie Tyrell on violin, and Patti Scialfa on background vocals, with Gary Mallaber on drums.

2. The title track returned to the set during the reunion tour as a blazing rocker, taken to a blistering, joyous extreme in several live versions featuring Tom Morrello from the political noise-rockers Rage Against the Machine sitting in on guitar. The words "holy fuck" don't really do these versions justice.

3. "Devils & Dust" was one of the newest songs on the album. It surfaced for the first time at the soundcheck for the *Rising* tour show in Vancouver in early 2003 and was the talk of the pit line that day. "All the Way Home," at the other extreme, was written

is a political song, rooted in the American war in the Gulf, while "Reno" is a sad, frank song about an encounter with a prostitute. "Leah" and "Long Time Comin'" are among Springsteen's finest adult love songs, but "Matamoros Banks" is very much in the social-observation mode common on *The Ghost of Tom Joad*.

For all that, *Devils & Dust* is a strong album, addressing a number of Springsteen's career- and lifelong concerns in highly distilled ways. The title song, for example, expresses his political leanings while never losing sight of the real individuals caught in the cross-fire of ideologies. "Long Time Comin'" is rooted in the reality of a long-term relationship and a promise to learn from the mistakes of the past.[4] "The Hitter" is a folk-music short story, rich in pathos and hard-won wisdom, about a boxer whose great talent is taking a fall. "Matamoros Banks" scratched Springsteen's socially conscious itch with its account of desperate Mexican immigrants drowning as they attempt to cross the titular river.[5]

And then there's "Jesus Was an Only Son."

The strands of faith and family that had run so deeply through Springsteen's work reached an apotheosis with "Jesus Was an Only Son," an account not only of Jesus's final hours, but also of the relationship between Christ and his mother. The song works on both levels, using imagery that is both domestic and canonical. A mother praying for her child is a powerful enough image, but it takes on a different hue when that child is Jesus. It's an intense, breathtakingly beautiful song.

---

for Southside Johnny in 1991. "Long Time Comin'" and "The Hitter" were both performed on the *Ghost of Tom Joad* tour in 1995 and 1996 (in fact, "The Hitter" lends its name to one of the best bootlegs from that tour, *The Hitter in Syracuse*.)

4. "I ain't gonna fuck it up this time" says as much with eight simple words—one of them an obscenity—as do whole songs on *Human Touch*. The line destroys me every time I hear it.

5. The song is beautiful, but also interesting from a stylistic perspective: the story unfolds in reverse, beginning with the body of an immigrant washed up on shore after several days in the river, and ending with the optimism of that same immigrant looking across the water at the land of plenty so agonizingly close.

Not that you would know it from the album proper. On *Devils & Dust*, "Jesus Was an Only Son" is a bit of a dud. It's listenable, but the musical setting is banal, and Springsteen's delivery is largely dispassionate, undermining the words and their significance. And this isn't just an instance where the live version of a song is better (more energetic, more intense) or different (with a recast musical setting, say). In the case of "Jesus Was an Only Son," the live version is a completely new song.

Typically, when Springsteen releases a song on a studio album, it remains largely fixed in that form; subsequent live versions might take a different musical approach, or contain minor lyrical variation,[6] but the song is "done." He's too much of a perfectionist to give early drafts the imprinteur of official release.[7]

It seems there was something about "Jesus Was an Only Son," though.

Perhaps it was the lyrics. Perhaps Springsteen felt he hadn't yet said what he actually wanted to say. Perhaps it was the experience of exploring the song for VH1 *Storytellers*.

Whatever the reason, throughout the *Devils & Dust* tour, "Jesus Was an Only Son" was a highlight, the quietest showstopper in the Springsteen canon.[8] Every night, he cracked the song open.

Early on, as he'd done on *Storytellers*, Springsteen interrupted the song with spoken word bits between the verses about what it

---

6. Probably my favorite of these is the shift in "Darkness on the Edge of Town," from "I lost my money when I lost my wife" to "I lost my faith when I lost my wife," which works better as a stand-alone and leads far more powerfully into the next line, "these things don't seem to matter much to me now."

7. This doesn't apply to collections like *Tracks* or *The Promise: The Darkness on the Edge of Town Story*, which are deliberate assemblages of such drafts. Also, Springsteen has historically had little problem with road testing and honing material before releasing it: the 1978 tour was highlighted by new songs like "Point Blank," "Independence Day," "Sherry Darling," and "The Ties That Bind," which wouldn't be released until *The River*.

8. The *Devils & Dust* tour was one of Springsteen's most controversial, and it had nothing to do with the music. Unlike the *Ghost of Tom Joad* tour in 1995, which had played intimate theatres—at a time in his career when Springsteen was somewhat out of

means to be a parent, and what it must have been like for Christ, imagining a life of running a seashore bar in Galilee, preaching on the weekends.[9] As the tour progressed, the song accreted meaning. Springsteen took to introducing the song by talking about his family, the Italian and the Irish sides, what it was like growing up in a small town in different shades of faith.[10] Within the song, he'd expand on his feelings about both parenthood and sacrifice.

By the time he hit Seattle and Vancouver in August 2005, the stories that accompanied the song had been developing for months. I had no idea. I'd kept myself largely ignorant of the format and the setlists for the shows, wanting to maintain a sense of suspense right up to the moment Springsteen took the stage.

Nothing could have prepared me anyway.

SUNDAY MORNING, a little past nine. There wasn't a car on the road, and the heat shimmered off the asphalt in gasoline waves as it stretched into the distance. Any dust I kicked up hung in the still air. God, it was hot. First thing in the morning and already my shirt was sticking to me. Again. How many times had I sweated through my clothes in the last twenty-four hours?

It was August 14, 2005, and I was walking down to my grandmother's house. She wanted to go to church, so if we were going to have a visit, just the two of us, it needed to be early. She'd baked

---

fashion—the 2005 tour was booked into arenas. Not, generally, full-size arenas; arenas that had been curtained to create more intimate spaces, but arenas nonetheless. The fans were, as one might expect, apoplectic, and they had a point. Having seen two of those shows, though, I can honestly say that Springsteen conquered the caverns. Of course, the fact that I was in the tenth and fourth rows might have something to do with that perception.

9. *Storytellers* included what must be a tremendous understatement for Springsteen: "Once you're a Catholic there's no getting out. That's all there is to it."

10. Later in the tour, a fan—who I know passingly in that Usenet newsgroup way—actually made up a map of Springsteen's neighborhood based on the story, using poster board and a Sharpie. If I recall correctly, Springsteen saw it in the audience one night, and took it from her, and proceeded to use it as a visual aid for the introduction not just that night but for the remainder of the tour.

muffins with fresh blueberries; they were waiting for me. She was waiting for me.

Cori and Xander were still asleep, snuggled together in the room that used to be Dave's, before that Mom and Dad's. Just across the hall from my old room, now given over to storage and garage sale finds.

My legs were killing me.

It feels sometimes like I've spent my whole life walking down that road. That morning, though, it all seemed different somehow. More real. I'd only had a couple of hours sleep—Greg had dropped me off pretty late after the concert—but I didn't feel tired, just different.

As different as everything around me.

I used to know everyone in all those houses. I was related to a lot of them. My Uncle Bill lived here, my Nanny, my great-grandmother, there, the Michaloskis across the street, the babysitter there. Now they're just houses, faces closed tight against the world, blinds drawn against the heat and the light of day.

I still flinch when I walk past the house where that fucking yellow dog used to live. Twenty-five years later, at age thirty-four, I caught myself walking on the other side of the highway, as far over on the shoulder, as close to the lip of the ditch, as I could.

Sunday morning, and it was so goddamn hot.

I wasn't used to the heat any more. I'd spent almost twenty years in Victoria, where even on the hottest days there's a breeze off the water, a hint of cool to stir the air. This dry, hanging heat...I hated it.

It was the only thing I hated at the moment, though. Which was, frankly, unusual for me.

Most days, I carried a lot of hate and anger, most of it directed at myself. Things weren't rosy, and they hadn't been for a while. I was tired all the time, working too hard and getting further and further behind. I was sick of never having enough money, never having enough time. My first book would be out in a year, and I was mired in revisions. I spent a lot of time wilfully not thinking about it.

That morning, though, I didn't really know what I was feeling. Open, maybe. Broken open.

Greg had picked me up in the middle of the afternoon the day before and we'd driven into Vancouver for the show. It was our second show in three days.

The Seattle show had blown my mind. Waiting for Greg and John to show up that day, I'd been part of a small crowd that thronged Springsteen outside the Key Arena's load-in area. I hadn't clambered to shake his hand or pushed anything in front of him to sign; I just hung near the back of the crowd and watched. And I was one of several people yelling for "Living Proof" when Springsteen asked the small crowd what folks wanted to hear.

He opened with the song that night. A song I never thought I would get to hear live, a song that was so important to me, and he opened with it. On the organ.

Seattle had been a mind-boggling, anything-can-happen kind of show. That was one of the benefits of it being a solo tour: there was no band to worry about; only one person on stage needed to know the songs.

Greg and I had both been buzzing about the Vancouver show as we drove into the city, as we had dinner, as we waited for the lights to go down.

In the fields at the side of the road I walked, the corn was high, the bright green of the sharp-edged leaves faded and heavy with dust. I wondered if it was Jubilee or one of the earlier varieties. If it was Jubilee it probably wouldn't be ready till close to mid-September, right around the time of the fall fair. If it was one of the earlier varieties, there had probably been some thirteen-year-old kid out in that field a few hours ago, just as the sun was coming up.

Springsteen had opened the Vancouver show with "Living Proof." The excitement that had dominated through the Seattle performance gave way, so I could actually listen to the song, hear the words. That first verse, which will always be about Xander to me. The next verses, about questioning your own life: "You do some sad,

sad things baby, when it's you you're trying to lose." And finally, the achingly beautiful last verse, with the family curled up together in one big bed, "a close band of happy thieves."

I cried.

The night had been full of moments to take your breath away, to break your heart.

The way Springsteen seemed to be singing the last verse of "Long Time Comin'" ("I ain't gonna fuck it up this time") to someone waiting in the wings, mere moments before he introduced his eldest son, Evan. Evan, about whom "Living Proof" had been written, was touring with his dad for a couple of weeks, playing guitar tech on his summer vacation.

There was the stark beauty of "The Rising," Springsteen backlit by a single, powerful spotlight so that his shadow seemed to fall over the whole arena as he sang, and the way he let the "dream of life" refrain build like a mantra, like a prayer.

There was that moment at the end of "This Hard Land," when he hit the line "if you can't make it stay hard, stay hungry, stay alive," and the house lights came up and the audience sang along. That one fragment as powerful as the whole of "Born to Run," for the same reasons.

There was the moment he sat down at the piano and started to play "The Promise," another song I never thought I would hear live. And hearing him start to sing "4th of July, Asbury Park (Sandy)," right after "Blinded by the Light"? I think that's why my throat was hurting, why I could barely speak that morning.

A train went by; the tracks ran along the far side of the cornfields. It churned up clouds of dust in its wake.

Growing up there, you got used to the trains. My grandmother used to greet one of her friends who worked on the passenger trains by leaning out her front window, waving two white napkins.

The sound of a train in the distance will always make me feel wistful, and make me feel at home: it's a cliché because it's true.

The night before, when Springsteen had started to talk about his family and the neighborhood he grew up in, I'd thought I was ready. But I had been undercut at every turn. "Living Proof," with its evidence of both a state of grace and hope for a future. Springsteen's son Evan, hearing his father's promise not to fuck up again. "Real World," a song not of defiance but of strength and acceptance.

Everything was about me, the whole show. Just as it was about every other person in that arena.

"Jesus Was an Only Son" destroyed me. It left me weak, and weeping in my seat. There was so much truth there. So much to consider. Parents, children. Men, women. Home, community. Responsibility, sacrifice.

When I was a kid, walking down to my grandmother's, I'd sometimes stop at Mrs. Clarke's place. It was just past the halfway point, and I'd ask to use her bathroom, but mostly I stopped because she usually had a cookie or a candy for me to take on my way.

Somebody else lives in Mrs. Clarke's house now; she died a few years ago.

Somebody else lives in Charlie's house now too. He died a while back.

Walking that highway, it's a walk into the past, and into the future.

But none of that mattered as I turned into the gravel driveway: my grandmother was waiting. And I knew that when I opened the door at the base of the back stairs, the air would be full with the smell of baking.

After the show, Greg and I were subdued. Sure, we went to a seedy bar: traditions must be observed. But we left pretty quickly.

We stopped at a Denny's just off the highway for pie and coffee.

There was a group of rowdy drunks across the restaurant, but we ignored them.

We were subdued. It's not that there was no post-show rush, it was just...different.

In the Circle, we talked about the show. We talked about our kids. We talked about our wives, our parents, our pasts, our hopes, and what we had lost along the way. We talked about our lives. There was no anger or rancor, just understanding and a hint of quiet sadness.

When Greg dropped me off at the house I grew up in, I undressed in the dark. My shirt had finally dried out, and I dropped it where I would be able to find it in the morning.

Xander was in bed with Cori, so I curled in behind him. He was cool and soft. I buried my face in his hair, my arm over him, my hand on Cori's side. I lay there in the dark, in the bedroom that had once been my mother and father's. There was a train in the distance, and I listened to my family breathe.

> I also figure that if our choices are given weight and meaning by the things that we sacrifice, and you choose some part of life, and you give up something else, I always figure Jesus had to be thinking about what he was going to lose. He must have been thinking, that Galilee… really nice this time of year. A little bar down by the beach, where they surely need somebody to manage the place. And Mary Magdalene, she could tend bar. You don't have to quit the preaching. You can just save it for the weekends. And they could have a bunch of kids. And get to see the sun fall on their face. And get to see the air fill their lungs at night when they're sleeping. And get to see the next day. And the next day. And the next day. And the next day…

Atlantic City

Album: *Nebraska*
Released: September 30, 1982
Recorded: January 3, 1982
Version discussed: "Atlantic City," performed by The Hold Steady[1]
Album/released: *War Child Presents Heroes*, February 16, 2009

THINGS TEND TO come full circle, if you step back far enough to see it.

Case in point: Bruce Springsteen.

Springsteen is a product of his age. He's spoken at length about the influence of The Beatles, and about how his life changed—as did the lives of so many in his generation—upon seeing the Fab Four on the *Ed Sullivan Show* for the first time. He's described the opening notes of Bob Dylan's *Like a Rolling Stone* as "that snare shot that sounded like somebody kicked open the door to your mind." He is a child of his time.[2]

---

1. I suppose I should say something about "Atlantic City," shouldn't I? Considering the way this chapter is going to go. Well, "Atlantic City" is one of Springsteen's strangest singles, and one of his best known songs. Drawn from the *Nebraska* album, it uses the crumbling excess of the Jersey waterfront gambling mecca to chronicle two lives of desperation and possible salvation. It's one of Springsteen's most covered songs, having appeared in versions by Pete Yorn, The Band, and Counting Crows, among others. The version by The Hold Steady appears on *Heroes*, a benefit compilation of covers raising funds for War Child.

2. Also helpful in this sort of trainspotting is to look at the covers Springsteen has chosen to perform over the course of his career, from warhorses like the "Detroit Medley" (made up generally of "Devil with a Blue Dress," "Good Golly Miss Molly,"

He is steeped in the music of the British Invasion—not just The Beatles and The Rolling Stones, but also The Animals and The Kinks—and in mid-sixties pop and soul. He came by his fondness for Elvis Presley through his mother's adoration, and his abiding passion for singers like Smokey Robinson and Sam Cooke is readily apparent. ("Mary's Place," from *The Rising*, for example, is clearly inspired by Cooke's "Meet Me at Mary's Place"). Springsteen has never made much of any inspiration he may have received from Van Morrison (aside from his early work with Them), but Morrison has staged decades of temper tantrums about being ripped off by the Boss; some of the songs on *The Wild, the Innocent & the E Street Shuffle* lend credence to his argument. Influences like Hank Williams and Johnny Cash can also be heard in Springsteen's music.

In time, Springsteen himself has become an inspiration. Putting aside his direct influence on fellow travelers like Southside Johnny and the Asbury Jukes, who came of age with Springsteen and for whom Springsteen wrote such songs as "The Fever" and "Hearts of Stone" (and with whom he shared the talents of Miami Steve Van Zandt), you can easily trace his influence on such rockers as U2 (in his typically understated fashion, Bono said of Springsteen, upon his induction into the Rock and Roll Hall of Fame, "Bruce has played every bar in the U.S.A., and every stadium. Credibility—you couldn't have more, unless you were dead. He's America's writer, and critic.") and The Clash (the late Joe Strummer wrote of Springsteen in 1997, "His music is great on a dark & rainy morning in England, just when you need some spirit & some proof that the big wide world exists the D.J. puts on 'Racing in the Streets' & life seems worth living again . . . life seems to be in cinemascope again.").[3]

Most interesting to me are the second generation of bands and songwriters to be inspired by Springsteen—my demographic

---

"C.C. Rider" and "Jenny Take a Ride"), The Beatles' "Twist and Shout," and Elvis Presley's "Can't Help Falling in Love," to more rarely performed numbers like The Animals' "It's My Life," Bob Dylan's "I Want You" and "Chimes of Freedom," Buddy Holly's "Rave On," and Chuck Berry's "Carol."

cohort, the performers who came of age with Springsteen-as-super-star, with *Born in the U.S.A.* and what followed.

The work of Counting Crows, for example, seems to grow organically out of an immersion in the music of Bruce Springsteen and Van Morrison. (Just think what Morrison would have to say about that.) Their first album, *August and Everything After* (which I consider to be one of the finest albums of the last twenty-five years) is steeped in that influence, with songs like "Round Here" echoing the existential anxiety of *Darkness on the Edge of Town* and their break-out single "Mr. Jones" giving the idea of rock and roll as salvation a radio-friendly sheen. "Rain King" strikes the delicate balance between defiance and surrender that runs through much of Springsteen's work, and in concert the song opens up to include snatches of Springsteen lyrics alongside the original words.[4]

Springsteen's importance to The Gaslight Anthem might be even more significant, though it's more subtle, at least sonically. The band members grew up in New Jersey and have remained there, even as they've found success in the last couple of years, and their music incorporates both the Jersey Shore sound (of which Springsteen is the prime exponent) and the boozy, punky swagger of Minneapolis's archetypal alt-rockers The Replacements. It might seem like an unwieldy blend, but The Gaslight Anthem makes it work; better, they make it sing. Their songs are hard-edged and propulsive—what Springsteen might have sounded like had he

---

3. The respect is clearly mutual: at the Grammy Awards in 2003, Springsteen and an ad hoc group that also featured Paul Simonon and Topper Headon of The Clash, Dave Grohl of Foo Fighters, Elvis Costello, and Miami Steve Van Zandt, performed the band's "London Calling" as a tribute to Joe Strummer.

4. There's a great video at countingcrows.com of a 2007 performance of "Rain King" that includes "Thunder Road" in its entirety. The band segues effortlessly into the Springsteen song, incorporating it into the musical setting of their original with a deftness that makes it seem as if "Thunder Road" had been there all along. The opening line, in singer Adam Duritz's voice, is surprising and heart-stopping every time, and the moment the band shifts from the climax of "Thunder Road" back into the climax of "Rain King" only ups the ante.

grown up listening to The Clash. Their records are strewn with references to Springsteen ("Meet Me by the River's Edge" on The '59 Sound, manages to name-check "No Surrender" and "Bobby Jean" in a single line, and "High Lonesome" riffs on "I'm On Fire" while also managing to quote from a Counting Crows song), but it's more a matter of sense, of feel. There's an urgent earnestness to The Gaslight Anthem, a fearless affixing of the band's heart to its sleeve, that is reminiscent of Springsteen in the mid-to-late seventies.

The sensibilities of Montreal-based art-arena rock collective Arcade Fire combine seventies art rock (including David Bowie, who has appeared with the band several times) and U2-style exuberance. (The Irish band used Arcade Fire's "Wake Up" as their entrance music during their Vertigo tour, and the Montreal band opened several dates for them.) You can hear the Springsteen influence, though, in songs like "Keep the Car Running" and "No Cars Go,"[5] and, more so, in their live performances. It's not just in the little things—bandleader Win Butler's nightly plunge into the audience to sing from the middle of the crowd harkens back to Springsteen's similar excursions during "Spirit in the Night" in the mid-seventies[6]—but in their overall presence live. There's a congregational aspect to the band's performances, a sense of communion and community that will be familiar to any Springsteen fan. Arcade Fire's goal, it seems, is to conquer any room they're in, no matter the size, and bring every audience member into each song: they're not performing for, they're performing with.[7]

Which brings me, inevitably, to The Hold Steady.

The Hold Steady seems equally inspired by early eighties punk

---

5. Yes, they're both car songs—I call 'em like I see 'em.
6. That bridging of the gap between performer and audience is one of many, many dazzling moments in the 1978 Houston concert video included in The Promise: The Darkness on the Edge of Town Story box set.
7. Two of my three major musical regrets for 2010 are my failure to venture across the strait to Vancouver to see shows by The Gaslight Anthem and Arcade Fire. The bruises I have from kicking myself may be permanent.

(including Hüsker Dü, who were local heroes when frontman Craig Finn was growing up in Minneapolis) and Springsteen.[8] They also have the work ethic down. Widely touted as the best bar band in America, The Hold Steady are constantly on the road, touring in support of a new album or in anticipation of the next. Their setlists are fluid, filled with rarities and well-chosen covers, though their favored covers come from either punk sources or seventies vintage arena rock.

And The Hold Steady are, like The Gaslight Anthem and Arcade Fire, part of a very small group of younger bands on whom Springsteen has bestowed his blessing. On the *London Calling: Live in Hyde Park* DVD, for example, you'll see Springsteen trading verses on "No Surrender" with Brian Fallon of The Gaslight Anthem. Their performance looks suspiciously like a passing of the torch, and they produce one of the finest versions of "No Surrender" I can recall hearing, to boot. There's also footage floating around of Springsteen guesting with The Gaslight Anthem, singing the chorus to their "The '59 Sound." Similarly, Springsteen and Arcade Fire have done guest spots at each other's concerts: Arcade Fire joining Springsteen on stage to sing "State Trooper," and Springsteen joining them on stage to sing "Keep the Car Running."

And The Hold Steady?

The impetus behind the *Heroes* compilation was for established rock icons, including Springsteen, Bob Dylan, Paul McCartney, and Leonard Cohen, to choose a song from their own catalogues and nominate a younger performer or band to cover it. Springsteen chose "Atlantic City" for The Hold Steady to cover. The song is a perfect choice: with its squalor and vague sense of impending doom, it fits well with The Hold Steady's own music.

---

8. The tension between influences in The Hold Steady's work is addressed, with typical flair, in "Barfruit Blues," a track from their first album *Almost Killed Me*: "half the crowd is calling out for born to run and the other half is calling out for born to lose. baby we were born to choose." You should be familiar with "Born to Run" by now; "Born to Lose" probably refers to the track by punk band Social Distortion.

THERE'S NOTHING, for a music fan, like the thrill of discovering a new hero. It's usually something that happens when you're a teenager.

From mumbling along with "Rosalita" to practicing my "Dancing in the Dark" moves in front of the full-length mirror in my mother's bedroom and listening to those bootleg tapes with Greg, devouring every word, every note, my discovery of Springsteen and his music had a visceral, physical effect on me. My heart expanded in my chest until it seemed close to bursting.

It was a lot like falling in love.

No, it was exactly like falling in love.

There are two sad things about that feeling, though.

The first is that you grow out of it.

As you get older, your reaction to music changes. For even the most dedicated music fan, the pleasure of a new discovery becomes less physical.[9] Your responses are cerebral, appreciative, rather than passionate.

I'm a huge Grateful Dead fan—they're playing as I write this—but I came to them too late. I love the music, I've read a lot about them, I've listened to concerts and watched DVDs, I've been immersed. But it's not the same.

I have a similar reaction to Pearl Jam. And to Tori Amos. Ryan Adams. The Black Crowes. The Drive-by Truckers. Richard Thompson.

I love them all, but I'm not *in* love with them, if you know what I mean.[10]

---

9. Two interesting exceptions to this, for me at least? Miles Davis and John Coltrane. I discovered jazz in my early twenties. Yet it took me a while to appreciate it, beyond the level of mood music. I reached a point, though, where it just... hit me. Listening to Davis's *Kind of Blue* or Coltrane's *A Love Supreme*? I get that feeling in my chest, that delicate balance between joy and weeping, every single time.

10. That being said, I do continue to have the experience of falling in love with individual songs. I may not be head over heels with The Black Crowes, but their "Soul Singing," well, it makes my soul sing. Lissie's cover of Kid Cudi's "Pursuit of Happiness" and Mumford & Sons' "Little Lion Man" both wrecked me this year, in that musical-punch-to-the-solar-plexus way that I so love.

The second sad thing about that feeling is that it's so easy to forget. As you get older, the sense of it slips away. If you're lucky enough to experience that passion again, though, it all comes rushing back.

Which is how I find myself pressed up against a stage in a sticky mob of bodies, soaked with sweat, empty beer cans scattered in front of me, my arms high in the air, my head thrown back in song.

It's August again, almost exactly five years after the Springsteen *Devils & Dust* concert, and I'm back in Vancouver for a show. It's not Springsteen this time, and I'm not at GM Place; this time it's the Vogue Theatre and The Hold Steady.[11] I'm surrounded by friends— Peter and Colin[12] and Lue, and Lue's friends Neil and Angela. It's as hot as an oven, and the music is loud enough to almost disappear into a wall of distortion. I'm as pissed as a newt, and I'm singing along with every word.

And I'm happy.

How did this happen? I'm turning forty in three months, and I'm completely lost over a band? That's not the usual way of things.

Screw the usual way.

I discovered The Hold Steady back in 2006, shortly after the release of their third album, *Boys and Girls in America*. I was drawn to them because of Craig Finn's way with a lyric: anybody who can reference Jack Kerouac in the opening line of a propulsive, desperate song like *Stuck Between Stations* ("there are nights when i think that sal paradise was right. boys and girls in america have

---

11. And the one thing I know, with dead certainty, is that they're absolutely not going to perform "Atlantic City." As far as I know, they've never performed it live. So yes, this whole "bonus track" thing is a bit of a bait-and-switch. Except for this: it really is a fabulous cover, and it definitely shows the role Springsteen has had in inspiring younger groups, and you shouldn't let the fact that I'm not really going to talk about it stop you from adding it to your version of this mix-tape. It really does round out the playlist nicely.

12. The trouble with this book ending in 2005 is that it lacks in any substantial Colin content. Colin's one of my closest friends, a fellow bookseller. As rare as it is to fall in love with a band in one's advancing years, it's rarer still to find a new true friend.

such a sad time together"[13]) was practically tailor-made for a book nerd like me.

Boys and Girls in America is a great album. The critics loved it, and l loved it, in that late-thirties sort of rational, appreciative way. I loved the album so much that I thought their next one, 2008's Stay Positive, was a disappointment. I played it a couple of times, liked it well enough, and then put it away. A while later, though, I gave it another try, playing it on my CD player in my office at the bookstore. I didn't listen to anything else for almost two months.[14]

I was having a hard summer, and Stay Positive, with its violence and heartbreak, its loss and pain, its overarching, fragile sense of hope, seemed to speak to something deep inside me.

The big moment didn't come until late September, though. I was standing outside the Doubletree Hotel in Seattle, across the street from Sea-Tac Airport—Cori, Xander, and I were down there to catch a musical, as I recall—having my last cigarette of the night. I was listening to a bootleg of a Hold Steady show from the week before, at the 40 Watt Club in Athens, Georgia, when the feeling came over me. It started in my chest, a surging, a heaving, a swelling that felt like it might crack my ribs. It traveled down my arms, down my legs, up my neck. I could barely suppress a sound midway between laughing and crying. I had to shake my head.

I'd never felt like that before.

Except... I had.

It all came back to me in a rush: the blanket on the beach, the heat of the sun, the taste of a lukewarm wine cooler, and Greg's shitty boom box playing that tape of Springsteen's 1978 Winterland

---

13. All of the lyrics in this section are by The Hold Steady, and are written by, in the most democratic band fashion, The Hold Steady.

14. A year after the album's release, almost to the day, I had the Stay Positive symbol—an infinity sign with a plus sign at the point where the circles touch—tattooed on the outside of my right wrist. I wanted it there not as a celebration of the band or the record, but as a reminder to myself to, well, stay positive. Has it worked? The jury, it seems, is still out.

show, more than three hours of breathless rock and roll, that feeling of instant connection and deep physical understanding.

Twenty years later, I was feeling it again.

After that, I dove headfirst into The Hold Steady. I bought their two earlier albums,[15] downloaded a bunch of shows. Every song spoke to me. Every song had lines that broke my heart.

The preceding months had been rough ones for me, full of lengthy, dark-hued introspection at every level: personal, professional, emotional. I had no idea how to balance the very real blessings of the life I had with the despair I always seemed to be feeling.

Into that emotional vortex came songs like "Lord, I'm Discouraged" ("excuses and half-truths and fortified wine"), "Constructive Summer" ("i went to yr schools, i did my detention, but the walls are so gray, i couldn't pay attention") and "Your Little Hoodrat Friend" ("it burns being broke and it hurts to be heartbroken but always being both must be a drag").[16] There was epic love and violence, emotional squalor, druggy highs, and bloody lows. Four albums' worth of people trying to find their way in their worlds, emerging bloody and sometimes broken if they emerged at all. It was so sad and hopeless, yet strangely redemptive and affirming, all wrapped up in hook-laden pop and bar-honed musical chops.

That November, Colin and I followed the band for a couple of nights. Seattle and Portland. Showbox SoDo and the Crystal Ballroom.

I was pretty drunk by the time the band opened that first show with "Citrus,"[17] and when Craig hit the line "lost in fog and love

---

15. I believe their second album, *Separation Sunday*, is one of the finest albums of the first decade of the new century. I could write a whole essay just on that.

16. You can see why lyrics like these, all credited just to The Hold Steady, would appeal to a word geek like myself.

17. Yes, you're noticing a trend: there's a close tie between Hold Steady shows and wilful public intoxication. (And for the record, it's not just us. The message boards are like scare stories for potential alcohol poisoning.) There's a line in "Constructive Summer,"

and faithless fear I've had kisses that make judas seem sincere," something inside me broke. That line cut through the questions and the pain and made me feel young and hopeful and free. It was cheaper than therapy. And then they kicked into "Stuck Between Stations" and it was like I exploded.

I emerged from that show drenched in whisky and Coke, throat torn apart, and mostly deaf in one ear.

I felt reborn.

I've seen The Hold Steady more times in the past two years than I've seen Springsteen in the last decade. Every show is different, and every show—every song—speaks to me in a different way.

What they have in common is what Craig says at the end of every show: "There is so much joy in what we do up here."

To see that joy, you need to find a clip of "Rosalita," from a Springsteen tribute show in April, 2007.[18] The event, a fundraiser, featured a healthy roster of musicians, including Ronnie Spector, Steve Earle, and Badly Drawn Boy, performing tracks from the Springsteen canon. The highlight, though, was Springsteen himself showing up to lead the musicians through a sloppy, passionate version of his perennial showstopper. The video is grainy and shaky, and the sound is poor, but that doesn't matter. What happened on that stage comes through.

The guy with the beard in the patterned blue shirt? The one who takes the first verse of the song? That's Craig. Keep your eye on him throughout the song, as he attempts to stay in the background, then gets called up to the mic again. Watch as he almost dissolves in happiness and abandon, completely losing any trace of self-consciousness.

---

the lead-off track from *Stay Positive*—"me and my friends are like double whisky coke no ice"—that Colin and I have taken to heart. Hard. It doesn't matter what we've been drinking at, say, the Lennox, all afternoon on the day of a concert: sometime before the show a couple of Jack and Cokes will magically arrive at the table, and Colin and I will toast and grin like the tweaked middle-aged rock geeks/teenage fangirls we are.

18. Oh, hell—we've come too far together for me to be coy now. It's on YouTube. You can find it by typing in "Rosalita Tribute."

When Finn tells the audience that "there is so much joy in what we do up here," this is what he's talking about.

There really is so much joy. That's what it's all about.

Let's face it—life can be pretty shitty. Often, at best, mind-numbingly routine.

But there are moments…

Some of them you see coming. The birth of your child. The sight of your soon-to-be-wife walking toward you on her father's arm. The first copy of your first book.

Other moments you just go with. You find the joy you can, and you hope it will sustain you through the dark.

That's why I'm here, pressed up against the stage, ears throbbing, hands sore from clapping, just about ready to fall over from drink.

This moment, right now.

The moment in "Your Little Hoodrat Friend" where Craig hits the lines "she's got blue black ink and it's scratched into her lower back. it said: 'damn right i'll rise again.' yeah, damn right you'll rise again," and everyone in the audience hits them with him.[19] I'm part of a sea of voices, a feast of friends. A Unified Scene.[20]

The moment when Craig sings my favorite lines from the new album, from a song called "The Smidge": "Make the sign of the cross with your cigarette. Come on, smudge a little smoke up in the night."

It's the moment that they finish the show with "Stay Positive," as if they knew it was exactly what I needed to hear.

Yes, there is so much joy.

---

19. Though the songs are all credited to The Hold Steady as a group, it's easy to slip into the assumption that the words are Craig's; there's an honesty and directness to them that is reminiscent of Springsteen at his best.

20. Ahem. Yes, there's a collective name. Like Tramps, some Hold Steady fans identify themselves with a phrase taken from one of the band's songs (well, two, actually): The Unified Scene. Yes, there are message boards. And yes, we all have nicknames (you kind of have to on a message board). And there are t-shirts. Not generic t-shirts, though. If you're a t-shirt Scenester, your shirt will have your number on it. And your nickname. It's like a team. Or a private club. Yes, I'm aware of how ridiculous that all sounds. It's also pretty cool. I'm very fond of my red Canadian-tour 2009 Scene shirt.

In this moment, for just this moment, I'm out of my own head. I'm feeling the music in my soul. The kick drum is catching the light and it looks like the beating of my heart. For this moment, for just this moment, everything is all right.

It's grace in 4/4 time, with a back beat and a guitar solo.

> ... *the kids at the shows,*
> *They'll have kids of their own,*
> *And the sing-along songs will be our scriptures.*
> "Stay Positive," THE HOLD STEADY

Bootleggers, Roll Your Tapes!

I'VE PLAYED IT a little coy in these pages on the whole subject of bootlegs. I am, to be frank, a bit conflicted. I recognize the moral question implicit in buying recordings of live shows at which recording is verboten. That being said, I wouldn't be the Springsteen fan I am today, and this book wouldn't exist, without bootlegs.[1]

So I leave it up to you. Here's a chronological list of ten of the finest recordings of Springsteen's career, bootlegs that have the potential to change your life.[2] In our wired age, you no longer need to frequent dodgy record stores or send money orders overseas: these recordings are all available for online download. (No, I won't say where.[3])

February 5, 1975 · The Main Point, Bryn Mawr, Pennsylvania
I discussed this bootleg at length in the "Thundercrack" chapter, but it's too good not to include on this list. It would be essential for the opening "Incident on 57th Street" alone, but the proto–"Thunder Road," with different lyrics, under the title "Wings for Wheels," is a

---

1   I am even more conflicted about studio bootlegs; to my mind, those tracks have been stolen, plain and simple, and were never intended for public consumption. That being said, yes, I have partaken. Yes, I did inhale.

2   In compiling this list, I thought it best to get some outside input, and I put the question of essential bootlegs out to my online community. I'm indebted to the members of the Facebook RMAS rebooted group for their input.

3   The shadiness of the bootleg world makes for a lot of confusion around releases, sound quality, sources, and so on. I've included a couple of variant titles, where applicable, for releases of some shows as guideposts. Your online sources will point you to the best available versions.

revelation, and the cover of Bob Dylan's "I Want You" is so beautiful and powerful that the mere thought of it makes me ache. If I could have only one bootleg, it would probably be this one. Released as *The Saint, the Incident and the Main Point Shuffle, You Can Trust Your Car to the Man Who Wears the Star*, and *Main Point Night.*[4]

August 15, 1975 (early show) · The Bottom Line, New York, New York

This FM broadcast from the ten-show Bottom Line stand at the height of the first burst of Bruce-mania (alongside the *Time* and *Newsweek* covers) revealed a band exploding with passion and drive, at once tightly controlled and risk-taking. The slow, almost sultry "The E Street Shuffle" includes the now-classic story of how the Big Man joined the band. The covers of "Then She Kissed Me," "When You Walk in the Room," and "Quarter to Three" are bar-band classics turned up to eleven, and "Born to Run" is fresh and intense in a way it has rarely been since. Released as *The Great White Boss* and *Live at the Bottom Line.*

December 15, 1978 · Winterland, San Francisco, California

I've said this before, but it bears repeating: there was a time when I wanted to collect every show from the 1978 tour. Choosing just one show for this list is a special kind of torture.[5] The Roxy show, the Passaic stand, the Agora concert—any one of them could be here. But for beginners, Winterland has it all: that long, delirious intro to "Prove It All Night"; a transcendent "Sad Eyes–Drive All Night" monologue in "Backstreets" that will take you out of your body; the rocking "Mona/The Preacher's Daughter/I Get Mad/ She's the One"... It will, I guarantee, blow your mind. There are many who believe this is perhaps the ultimate Springsteen bootleg: I'm one of them. Released as *Live in the Promised Land* and *Winterland Night.*

---

4   Among the foremost bootleg labels of the last decade or so is Crystal Cat: their recordings and releases are generally top-notch. Their releases all follow the (blank) *Night* format, so there's a hint.

5   A *Sophie's Choice* analogy would be excessive, but only just.

December 31, 1980 · Nassau Coliseum, Uniondale, New York

One of the longest, and finest, Bruce Springsteen shows in the canon. The band rings in the new year, and the new decade, with thirty-eight songs, including the only performance of "Held Up Without a Gun." The energy is over the top, and this one is absolutely essential. Some recordings include the pairing of "Incident on 57th Street" and "Rosalita (Come Out Tonight)" from the previous night, the only time the songs were performed as they appear on the album prior to the "whole album" shows of 2009. Wow. Just...wow. Released as *In the Midnight Hour* and *Nassau Night*.

July 13, 1984 · Alpine Valley Music Theater, East Troy, Wisconsin

A sentimental favourite, this show was one of the first bootlegs I owned, and it stands the test of time. With a roaring "Born in the U.S.A.," a mini-set of *Nebraska* tracks, a goofy "Pink Cadillac," and a fantastic cover of the Rolling Stones' "Street Fighting Man," this is a perfect representation of the early *Born in the U.S.A.* tour. Released as *Alpine Valley* and *Alpine Valley Night*.

May 3, 1988 · Shoreline Amphitheater, Mountain View, California

This is the show that formed the background music to that conversation in the "Brilliant Disguise" chapter, and it captures the early stages of the *Tunnel of Love* tour, complete with horn section. "Rosalita" was back in the setlist. The opening pairing of "Tunnel of Love" and B-side "Be True" set the emotional tone for the show. The sweet, wistful "All That Heaven Will Allow," complete with Springsteen and Clemons's park bench–set intro, is charming and affecting, while "Spare Parts" is a raging, cathartic burst. It's a fantastic show, and a fantastic tour. Released as *Roses and Broken Hearts*.

November 16–17, 1990 · Shrine Auditorium, Los Angeles, California

I wrote about these two shows earlier, the benefits for the Christic Institute that saw Springsteen break his post–*Tunnel of Love* seclusion. But it bears repeating: these are absolutely essential recordings, and they justify the entire bootleg industry. The shows are stark, solo, and acoustic, with breathtaking moment after breathtaking moment. The first-ever performances of "Real World" are the sound of a man coming to terms with himself in public, while "Redheaded Woman" is a playful bit of exhibitionism. The recasting of older material, including "Thunder Road" and "Brilliant Disguise," reveals heretofore unexplored depths, and even the usually triumphant "Tenth Avenue Freeze-Out" takes on a mournful tone.[6] Released as *Acoustic Tales* and *Christic Night*.

November 8, 1996 · St. Rose of Lima School, Freehold, New Jersey

The two finest shows of *The Ghost of Tom Joad* tour are the most atypical. The November 26, 1996, show at the Paramount Theater in Asbury Park, N.J., was a homecoming of sorts, with a wildly varied setlist and guest appearances by Danny Federici, Little Steven Van Zandt,[7] and "Mad Dog" Vini Lopez. I, however, lean toward the November 8 show in Freehold as one of the most significant nights of Springsteen's performing career. Highlights include one of the few performances of "In Freehold," and a personal setlist that presents a vivid picture of Springsteen's life to that point. Ah, hell, get 'em both. November 26 released as *Asbury Park Night*; November 8 released as *Freehold Night*.

AFTER THE turn of the millennium, two things happened that have substantially reduced the importance of commercial bootlegging over the last decade. The first was a certain looseness in Springsteen's regard for his work. Tours since the reunion tour are largely well represented with official releases: the *Live in Barcelona*, *Live in Dublin*, and *London Calling Live in Hyde Park* DVDs are solid shows

---

6   It was the Christic version of "Tenth Avenue Freeze-Out," with the sad refrain of "I'm on my own, and I can't go home," that I played over and over the night Clarence Clemons died. It broke my heart.

7   After leaving the E Street Band in 1984, Van Zandt underwent a nicknamectomy, replacing "Miami Steve" with "Little Steven." His band in those years was called Little Steven and the Disciples of Soul.

from the *Rising*, *Seeger Sessions*, and *Working on a Dream* tours, respectively. The second was the rise in technology: the presence of the internet in every home and the ubiquity of recording devices—audio and video—pretty much put professional bootleggers out of business. Virtually every show is now recorded and distributed online within hours of the final bows. There are a couple of fan-created projects, however, that are well worth seeking out:

The Promise Delivered

The final stand of the 1999–2000 reunion tour at New York City's Madison Square Garden is captured officially on the *Live in New York City* CDs and DVDs, but this seven-disc fan project is worth tracking down. The first three discs capture the final night, July 1, 2000, in its entirety. If the crowd chanting "E Street Band, E Street Band" late in the show doesn't bring a lump to your throat, you're clearly doing something wrong. And the rewritten "Blood Brothers" that closed out the night, and the tour, will make any Springsteen fan cry. Discs four through six capture rarities and one-offs from the stand. The seventh disc, a data disc, is a bit of a relic now, but this collection is essential.

Love, Tears and Mystery

The solo acoustic 2005 *Devils & Dust* tour isn't universally adored by fans, but, personally, I find it a revelation, night after night. The eleven-disc *Love, Tears and Mystery* compilation exhaustively captures that tour. The first two discs are a "typical" set[8] compiled from a variety of sources, while the next nine discs (yes, nine) capture every song performed on the tour, along with variant versions ("Born in the U.S.A." with regular mic and with distorting bullet mic, for example). Is there such a thing as too exhaustive? Maybe, but this isn't it. *Love, Tears and Mystery* is a labour of love, and it's

---

8   There's no such thing as a "typical" *Devils & Dust* show, but the concerts followed a general format, which the first two discs document.

probably the bootleg I've listened to most in the last five years. There is much, much here to love.

SPRINGSTEEN HAS been performing for over forty years; these recordings are, of course, just the tip of the iceberg. A taster, as it were. If you like these, there's a lot more out there—some better shows, some better sound, buried treasures, and colossal performances. Download speeds are fast, and hard drives are cheap: roll your tapes!

Sources

Bruce Springsteen: Official Site. Located at brucespringsteen.net.

Calvi, Paolo, et al. Killing Floor: Bruce Springsteen Database. Located at brucespringsteen.it.

Cavicchi, Daniel. *Tramps Like Us: Music and Meaning among Springsteen Fans.* New York: Oxford University Press, 1998.

Coles, Robert. *Bruce Springsteen's America: The People Listening, a Poet Singing.* New York: Random House, 2003.

Cross, Charles, et al. *Backstreets: Springsteen, the Man and His Music.* New York: Harmony Books, 1991.

Diomedi, David, director. VH1 *Storytellers: Bruce Springsteen.* 2005.

Editors of Rolling Stone, ed. *Springsteen: The Rolling Stone Files.* New York: Hyperion, 1996.

Eliot, Marc. *Down Thunder Road: The Making of Bruce Springsteen.* London, UK: Plexus, 1992.

Guterman, Jimmy. *Runaway American Dream: Listening to Bruce Springsteen.* Cambridge, MA: Da Capo Press, 2005.

Henke, James. "Bruce Springsteen: The Rolling Stone Interview." *Rolling Stone,* August 6, 1992.

Kirkpatrick, Rob. *Magic in the Night: The Words and Music of Bruce Springsteen.* New York: St. Martin's Griffin, 2009.

Landau, Jon. "Growing Young with Rock and Roll." *The Real Paper,* May 22, 1974.

Masur, Louis P. *Runaway Dream: Born to Run and Bruce Springsteen's American Vision.* New York: Bloomsbury Press, 2009.

Polizzotti, Mark. *Highway 61 Revisited.* New York: Continuum, 2006.

Sandford, Christopher. *Springsteen: Point Blank*. London, UK: Warner, 2000.

Sawyers, June Skinner, ed. *Racing in the Streets: The Bruce Springsteen Reader*. New York: Penguin, 2004.

Springsteen, Bruce. *Bruce Springsteen: Songs*. New York: Avon, 1998.

Wieder, Judy. "Bruce Springsteen: The *Advocate* Interview." *The Advocate*, April 22, 1996.

Zimny, Thom, director. *Wings For Wheels: The Making of Born to Run*. 2005.

Zimny, Thom, director. *The Promise: The Making of Darkness on the Edge of Town*. 2010.

Acknowledgements

ACKNOWLEDGEMENTS ARE A tricky thing: on the one hand, they're vaguely self-indulgent, and most people don't read them. On the other hand, to a lot of the people who do read them, they're important, and not an indulgence on my part at all.

Some things just need to be said.

I usually start my acknowledgements pages with a caveat, and it's even more important with this book: the things I got right, I had a lot of help with. Any mistakes are entirely my own.

This might sound corny, considering this whole book is an acknowledgement of sorts, but it needs to be said: Bruce? Thank you for everything.

I'd like to thank Rob Sanders, who asked me to write this book, and the folks at Greystone, who worked with me on making it a reality.

I'd like to thank my editor, Barbara Pulling, for whipping my prose and punctuation into shape, and curbing some of my excesses, and my copy editor, Pam Robertson, for saving me from myself.

I'd like to thank my agent, Anne McDermid, and her associates, all of whom remain utterly unfazed when I throw curveballs their way.

I'd like to thank Anne Collins, my publisher at Random House, for her understanding and flexibility when it comes to projects like this.

I'd like to take a moment to recognize and thank the massive community of Bruce Springsteen fans around the world. There is no fact so hidden that someone doesn't know it, no magazine article so old that someone can't find it, no setlist so obscure that someone can't talk about it. I can't express how much I appreciate being the beneficiary of that accrued knowledge—I really couldn't have written this book without it.

It's more than knowledge, though: it's genuine community, and I'm thrilled to be a part of it.

This being in part a memoir, I am indebted to the understanding and support of the people I've written about. Peter and Greg, my friends, my brothers, thank you. Not just for the book—for everything. Drinks are on me, when we three meet again.

There are a lot of other people in this book, as well. Family, friends from the various times of my life, acquaintances, and strangers—I am indebted to you all. As I was writing, I was careful to tell my stories, and avoid those that weren't mine to tell. I hope that nothing in these pages gives offense, or causes pain—that was certainly not my intention.

I am indebted to my early readers. Deep thanks to my mother, Greg, Peter, Colin, Clare, Stacey May, and Athena for their insights and support.

CLOSER TO HOME...

A considerable debt of gratitude to Domenique Rosenblum for her patience and understanding. A struggling writer has never had a better landlady.

Xander, thank you. I know you understand what it's like to be bubbling over with an obsession. You're not that pointy-headed little baby any more, and I didn't realize, as overwhelmed and blown away as I was the day you were born, that those feelings wouldn't fade, that they'd grow stronger every day.

And Cori.

It's a cliché to say that words don't do something justice, but anyone who's read this far knows that "thank you" is really insufficient when it comes to you, Cor. For more than two decades you've been with me every step of the way, and I shudder to think of how those years would have been, who I would have become, without you.

I've said it before and I stand by it: you're the strongest woman I know. This book was a hard one, on a number of levels, and you never flinched. Knowing that even when things are rough we can meet across a page—yours or mine—means more to me than I can express. You have always been, and remain, my first reader, my fiercest champion, my wisest critic. In these, and so many other ways, I am blessed to have you in my life.

ROBERT J. WIERSEMA is an independent book-seller, a reviewer who contributes regularly to several national newspapers, and the best-selling author of two novels: *Before I Wake* and *Bedtime Story*. He lives in Victoria, British Columbia.